Bringing
Sons to Glory

Dewey (Bud) Gardner

Bringing Sons to Glory
by Dewey (Bud) Gardner

Printed in the United States of America

ISBN 9781612155708

www.xulonpress.com

Endorsement for book "Bringing Sons to Glory" by Dewey E. Gardner (Brother Bud)

The eager heart of every sincere son or daughter of the Most High God has an unconquerable desire to know what is deep in the heart of the Father! This book reveals that deep secret to each of us – Bringing Sons to Glory - and then delivers the quiet confidence that the Holy Spirit is able to perfect such a work within us. I'm convinced that this book will revolutionize your life and ministry!

Pastor Charles E. Flowers
Senior Pastor of Faith Outreach Center, Int'l
President of the Gathering of Pastors & Leaders
of San Antonio
President of the Association of Churches of San Antonio
Convener of Congress for Life of San Antonio

Contents

Preface

My prayer for those who read this small contribution to the vast multitude of books written on marvelous themes found in God's holy Word is that you read this small book meditatively and with an open heart. The author is fully aware of his fallibility. There may be some things on which we disagree.

However, my prayer is that you not read through these pages as a critic, but as one hungering for holiness. If, after a diligent search for something to help you in your quest for God, and, finding no help here, reread these pages with the red pen in hand.

You are probably already aware that the Bible is a spiritual Book. Spiritual truth may be delivered in imperfect vessels. Pearls of great price may be produced in ugly oysters.

Trust the Holy Spirit to deliver the message to the heart. He is able to guide you into all truth and help sort out error.

It is recommended these pages be read in the light of what was spoken to the Corinthians by the apostle Paul,

"And I, brethren, when I came to you, did not come with excellence of speech or of wisdom declaring to you the testimony of God. For I determined not to know anything among you except Jesus Christ and Him crucified. I was with you in weakness, in fear, and in much trembling. And my speech and my preaching were not with persuasive words of human wisdom, but in demonstration of the Spirit and of power, that your faith should not be in the wisdom of men but in the power of God." (1 Cor. 2:1-5)

Introduction

"For it became him, for whom are all things, and by whom are all things, in bringing many sons unto glory, to make the captain of their salvation perfect through sufferings" (Heb. 2:10).

Here is something that staggers the imagination – out of this sinful, degenerate, degraded, deplorable human race, God is "bringing many sons unto glory."

What is this "bringing sons unto glory?" Surely it is more than just taking people to heaven. The life beyond is a glorious existence. In 1 Corinthians 15 we read that just as the stars differ one from another in glory, so is the resurrection of the saints. Paul wrote that those who are joint heirs with Christ, who suffer with Him, will be glorified together with Him (Rm. 8:17) and that there is a glory that shall be revealed in us (Rm. 8:18). Peter also wrote that we are called to glory and virtue (2 Peter 1:3).

Christ is sanctifying and cleansing the church by the washing of water by the word, that He might present it to Himself a glorious church (Eph 5:26, 27). John saw in a vision the holy city New Jerusalem (which the angel seems to identify as the Bride of Christ) descending from God out of heaven, having the glory of God (Rev. 21:10, 11).

Bringing sons to glory is a process. The beginning of the process is the Son of God becoming the Son of Man. Deity became man (See 1 Tim. 3:16). Through this great mystery the Only Begotten partook of flesh and blood (identifying with the human race) and through death and resurrection became the Firstborn. In this glorious beginning, God redeemed us to Himself and began the process by which He brings many sons unto glory, the glory of being joint heirs with Christ.

Just as the First born learned obedience by the things which he suffered (Heb. 5:8) and as captain of our salvation, was made perfect through suffering (Heb. 2:10), so must those who are the heirs of salvation pass through many learning experiences in the process of being brought unto glory.

This book is designed to explore this experience and explains how they "work together for good to them that love God, and are the called according to His purpose."

In developing our theme we will be able to discover things that inhibit the process and things that enhance our progress. Inhibitors become stumbling blocks and enhancers become stepping stones. We must know the difference that we may shun one and embrace the other.

We will also find answers to some perplexing questions such as: who is Satan and why is he allowed to roam about in God's creation? What is the mystery of iniquity and why is it allowed to operate? What is the flesh that lusts against the spirit? How can God allow men to have freedom and yet maintain absolute control? What is the difference between the world that God loves and the world we are commanded to not love? Why must we not love the world? How do we, as believers, overcome the world, the flesh and the devil? What are the eternal consequences of overcoming?

May God give us a Spirit of revelation and increase our understanding in these things that we may glorify Him by exhibiting His glory.

Chapter One

Bringing Sons to Glory

What on earth is God doing? Can we know what our awesome God is up to? The question pertains to what God is doing on this planet earth. God, considering Who He is, may be involved in more things than we could possibly imagine. We can know, and we need to know what God is doing among men. If we do not know what God is doing we may be opposing instead of cooperating with Him.

The answer to the question is many fold. God is involved in many things on earth and we may be and we should be involved with Him in more than one of these.

But the Bible reveals what the number one thing is that God is doing on earth today. Certainly God is seeking and saving the lost, He is destroying the works of the devil, He is blessing men with great goodness, but none of these (as important and wonderful as they are) are the number one thing God is doing. All these are part of and the means to God's revealed purpose.

> Ephesians 1:9-10 states, "having made known to us the mystery of His will, according to His good pleasure which He purposed in Himself, that in the dispensation of the fullness of the times He might gather together in one all things in Christ, both which are in heaven and which are on earth – in Him."

Here we are told what God's purpose has been from the beginning – to bring everything in heaven and earth (with the exception of Himself under the Headship of Jesus Christ. All this was planned and purposed from the very beginning. This is God's Ultimate Purpose.

Anyone who believes in God at all must believe that He knows what is coming before it happens. James, an apostle in Jerusalem, said, "Known to God from eternity are all His works" (Acts 15:18). Peter, referring to the crucifixion of our Lord, states, "Him (Jesus) being delivered by the determined purpose and foreknowledge of God, you have taken by lawless hands, have crucified, and put to death."

This tells us that God not only knew what was coming, but it was by His "determined purpose". We believe in God with whom nothing is impossible. He plans, He purposes and He performs His will. Isaiah 46:9, 10 declares, "I am God, and there is no other; I am God, and there is none like Me, declaring the end from the beginning, and from ancient times things are not yet done, saying, My counsel shall stand, and I will do all my pleasure."

God's original purpose, which is to bring everything under the Headship of Jesus Christ, was purposed in Himself before laying the foundations of the universe. To guarantee success in accomplishing His purpose, He purposed it in Himself. In other words, for His purpose to fail, God must fail – which is an impossibility.

"The Lord of hosts has sworn, saying, Surely, as I have thought, so it shall come to pass, and as I have purposed, so it shall stand; For the Lord of hosts has purposed, and who shall disannul it? His hand is stretched out, and who shall turn it back" (Isaiah 14:24, 27).

Let us reason together now. Why did God begin all of this in the first place Was it not in order to bring into existence a being, like unto Himself (not equal to, but of the same type) with whom He could fellowship?

Was God lonely before He created man? Of course not! How could the all sufficient God need anything? The Father, Son and Holy Spirit had sweet and complete fellowship within Himself. He needed nothing! It was His choice to do what He did. He did it because He wanted to.

What did He do? He, in His divine ingenuity created this entire universe (with all its vastness and every creature in it) in order to bring man into existence. (Not as he now is, but as he shall be when God is finished with him). Angels, though holy living beings who have ability to communicate, could not be what God created man to be. They are ministering spirits to minister for those who are the heirs of salvation.

Man's destiny is to be above cherubim, angels and archangels and every other created being. Such lofty reasoning brings us to exclaim with the Psalmist, "When I consider your heavens, the work of your fingers, the moon and the stars, which you have ordained, what is man that you are mindful of him, and the son of man that you visit him? For you have made him a little lower than the angels (*Heb. Elohim*) and you have crowned him with glory and honor. You have made him to have dominion over the works of your hands; you have put all things under his feet" (Ps. 8:3-6).

Now let us come to the subject of this book "Bringing Sons To Glory." It is obvious "God is not finished with us yet". But let us be assured "He who has begun a good work in you will complete it until the day of Jesus Christ" (Phil. 1:6).

God's determined purposed (to bring everything under the headship of Christ), involves bringing His sons to glory. Hebrews 2:10, 11 informs us that God is "bringing many sons to glory".

What is the glory to which these sons of God are being brought? Is it not the glory of the Christ life within them and the glory to which they are called at His coming and kingdom (1 Thess. 2:12)? The Christ life within the sons is being progressively revealed as "we all, with unveiled face, beholding as in a mirror the glory of the Lord, are being transformed into the same image from glory to glory, just as by the Spirit of the Lord" (2 Cor. 3:18). The final stage of this transformation of our mortal bodies is "the redemption of our body" (Rm. 8:23), at the return of Christ.

It might help if we think of this more as being in a glorious existence rather than being in a glorious place. Heaven is a glorious place, but it is glorious because of the glorious beings that dwell there. God (Father, Son, and Holy Spirit) is the most glorious of Beings. Now that Jesus (God made flesh) has been raised from the dead by the glory of the Father (Rm. 6:4), He is a glorious man. That is the glory into which sons are being brought. As we behold His glory we are being transformed into the same image from glory to glory, even as by the Holy Spirit (2 Cor. 3:18).

The sons who suffer with Christ also share in His glory at His coming and His kingdom, "For I consider that the sufferings of this present time are not worthy to be compared with the glory which shall be revealed in us. For the earnest expectation of the creation eagerly waits for the revealing of the sons of God" (Rm. 8:18, 19).

God first works for the sons by taking care of the sin problem, He then works within them to make them Christlike, and then He works through them to accomplish His purpose.

Peter tells us we are called to glory and virtue (excellence) (2 Pet. 1:3). He also assures us that when we endure fiery trials for Christ's sake the Spirit of glory and of God rests upon us. "Beloved, do not think it strange concerning the fiery trial which is to try you; but rejoice to the extent that you partake of Christ's suffering, that when His glory is revealed you may also be glad with exceeding joy.

If you are reproached for the name of Christ, blessed are you for the Spirit of glory and of God rests upon you" (1 Pet. 4:`12-14).

The ultimate glory of the sons will be when the sons are "revealed" at the second coming of Christ – not just that they appear glorious, but they will reign with Him in His glorious kingdom. Hallelujah!

We are told in Romans 8:28, 29 (Amplified) "We are assured and know that [God being a partner in their labor] all things work together and are [fitting into a plan] for good to and for those who love God and are called according to [His design and purpose].

For those whom He foreknew [of whom He was aware and loved beforehand], He also destined from the beginning [foreordaining them] to be molded into the image of His Son [and share inwardly His likeness], that He might become the firstborn among many brethren".

The term "firstborn" means "priority to and preeminence over". Christ is the Firstborn among many brethren. There are other sons in the category referred to in this passage. Jesus is the first and highest, there are others like Him (in the same class, but not equal to Him).

There are four categories in which Christ is called the Firstborn. We will consider these in order of their occurrence and explain the significance of each.

The term is used of Christ in Colossians. "He is the image of the invisible God, the firstborn over all creation. For by Him all things were created that are in heaven and that are on earth, visible and invisible, whether thrones or dominions or principalities or powers. All things were created through Him and for Him. And He is before all things, and in Him all things consist" (Col. 1:15-17).

The Firstborn refers to His relationship to the Father. Before the beginning began He had already existed as the One having priority to and preeminence over all of creation. This in no way infers He Himself had a beginning. It was He who began the beginning. He existed eternally as the Word of God. "In the beginning was the Word, and the Word was with God, and the Word was God. He was in the beginning with God. All things were made through Him, and without Him nothing was made that was made" (Jn. 1:1-3).

Not only is the Firstborn before the beginning, but the Word that was "with God, and was God "became man". And the Word became flesh and dwelt among us, and we beheld His glory, the glory as of the only begotten of the Father, full of grace and truth" (Jn. 1:14).

"And she (Mary) brought forth her firstborn Son and wrapped Him in swaddling cloth…" (Lk. 2:7). In this passage, He is the firstborn of Mary. He is Seed of the woman whose heel would be bruised by Satan, but Who would bruise Satan's head in the process (Gen. 3:15). The conception and birth of this Child through Mary was no ordinary birth. Mary, upon being told by the angel that she would bear a child, inquired of the angel how this could be, seeing she had not had sexual relations with a man. (The normal and ordinary way of conceiving).

The explanation given by the angel is truly awe inspiring. This was to be a miracle birth. The Holy Spirit would come upon Mary, the power of the Highest would overshadow her; she would conceive in her womb, and the Son of God would be born. Mary believed the word (Lk. 1:45), presented herself to the Lord (Lk.1:38), and the Miracle child was born. "She brought forth her firstborn son….." (Lk. 2:7).

This is a much greater miracle than that a woman conceived and produced a child without the joining of the male and female elements which combine to reproduce human life. It is the miracle of joining the elements of God with that of the female to bring forth the God Man!

Jesus embodied in Himself all that makes God God and (at the same time) all that makes man man.

Jesus is God incarnate. In Matthew 1:20, 21 We are told the angel comforted Joseph, husband to be of Mary (who was pregnant), by saying to him that that which is conceived in her was of the Holy Spirit, and that he (Joseph) was to name Him Jesus. To answer all speculation for all time as to whether or not He was God, we are told this: "So all this was done that it might be fulfilled which was spoken by the Lord through the prophet saying: 'Behold, the virgin shall be with child, and bear a Son, and they shall call his name Immanuel' which is translated 'God with us'" (Mt. 1:20-23).

Is His name "Jesus" or is it "Immanuel"? He is called Jesus (Savior) because that is what He does. He saves His people from their sins. He is Immanuel (God with us) because that is what He is in His essential being.

He did not stop being God when He became man. He is altogether God and He is altogether man. Paul wrote to

Timothy, "And without controversy great is the mystery of godliness: God was manifested in the flesh" (1 Tim. 3:16).

As the firstborn son of Mary, Jesus is all God intended man to be while in the fleshly body. In redemption Christ restores man to the original state so that, by His life in us, we can live as God intended (more on this later).

We read in the Gospel of John 1:14 that when the Word was made flesh, they beheld His glory, glory as of the only begotten of the Father, full of grace and truth. Jesus did not walk around every day with a glowing halo about His head. (Though three of His followers saw Him shine brightly on the Mount of Transfiguration. They were given a glimpse of what was to be revealed eventually.)

This Son of God/Son of Man was truly glorious. Peter, one of those on the Mount of Transfiguration says, "We did not follow cunningly devised fables when we made known to you the power and coming of our Lord Jesus Christ, but were eyewitnesses of His Majesty. For He received from God the Father honor and glory when such a voice came to Him from the Excellent Glory "This is my beloved Son, in whom I am well pleased" (2 Pet. 1:16, 17). The same apostle testified, "The Word which God sent to the Children of Israel – He is Lord of all - that word you know, which was proclaimed throughout all Judea, and began from Galilee after the baptism which John preached: how God anointed Jesus of Nazareth with the Holy Spirit and with power, who went about doing good and healing all who were oppressed by the devil, for God was with Him" (Acts 10:38).

Jesus is not only the Eternal Firstborn, and Mary's firstborn, He is also the Firstborn of the resurrection. "And He is the head of the body, the church, who is the beginning, the firstborn from the dead, that in all things He may have the preeminence" (Col. 1:18). (See also Rev. 1:5)

Being the Firstborn from the dead makes Him the Glorious Head of a totally new race of man. He is its Originator, Leader and Life Source.

Through His death, burial and resurrection, Jesus ended one race of human beings, and created a totally new race. By so doing He made the first race (the old man) obsolete. God did not change the old man into the new, He crucified and buried him. In His resurrection He created a totally new man. All this was done through the act of substituting His only begotten son Jesus for the old corrupt man Adam.

Adam, the man of earth, had corrupted his way by becoming self centered instead of God centered. In this self centered state of corruption Adam brought forth after his kind.

Jesus, the heavenly man, (the Lord from heaven) brings forth after His kind. The second man (The Lord from heaven) is God's ultimate intention. This was the Man God intended from the beginning. The question may be asked, "Then why did not God just create that man in the first place?

In order to have the man He envisioned, God must first create natural man. He had already created spirit beings but they were for another purpose than that of man. The man God purposed was to be above these ministering spirits (See Hebrews 1:14). Man is destined to be in the same classification as God (like God but not equal to Him). It was intended from the beginning that God and man would be joined together in Jesus Christ.

"Just as He chose us in Him before the foundation of the world, that we should be holy and without blame before Him in love, having predestined us to adoption as sons by Jesus Christ to Himself, according to the good pleasure of His will. Having made known to us the mystery of His will, according to His good pleasure which He purposed in Himself, that in the dispensation of the fullness of the times He might gather together in one all things in Christ, both which are in heaven and which are on earth—in Him. In Him also we have obtained an inheritance, being pre-destined according to the purpose of Him who works all things according to the counsel of His will" (Eph. 1:4, 5; 9-11).

For all this to become reality, it was necessary that natural man be created.

"And so it is written, "The first man Adam became a living being." The last Adam became a life-giving spirit. However, the spiritual is not first, but the natural, and afterward the spiritual. The first man was of the earth, made of dust; the second Man is the Lord from heaven. As was the man of dust, so also are those who are made of dust; and as is the heavenly Man, so also are those who are heavenly. And as we have borne the image of the man of dust, we shall also bear the image of the heavenly Man" (1 Cor. 15:45-49).

God did not plan for man to sin, but He had anticipated it and prepared for it. The New Testament is the gospel account of God's miraculous solution to the problem of sin. (The process by which God ended the old man in Adam and created a new man in Christ is explained more fully in Chapter Six and Seven.)

For our current discussion of how God is bringing many sons to glory, let us accept the Biblical fact that the old man in Adam was crucified (as far as God is concerned) when Jesus was crucified and buried with Him, and that the new man was created in Christ when He was raised in newness of life as the "life giving Spirit" (1 Cor. 15:45-49).

The natural man must be transformed into the spiritual man in order to inherit the kingdom of God (1 Cor. 15:50). This transformation is finalized either by dying in Christ or by the power of the Holy Spirit in the rapture.

Even Jesus, who had entered the race of natural men through the virgin (Mary), died (but not for His own sin).

"And as it is appointed for man to die once, but after this the judgment, so Christ was offered once to bear the sins of many. To those who eagerly wait for Him He will appear a second time, apart from sin, for salvation" (Heb. 9:27, 28).

The Man Christ Jesus who became the "Life Giving Spirit" in the resurrection has given to us His Holy Spirit. "For God did not call us to uncleanness, but in holiness. Therefore he who rejects this (holiness) does not reject man, but God, who has given us His Holy Spirit" (1 Thes. 4:7,8).

The Holy Spirit, the Spirit of Holiness, is the Spirit of life in Christ Jesus.

"For the law of the Spirit of Life in Christ Jesus has made me free from the law of sin and death. For what the law could not do in that it was weak through the flesh, God did by sending His own Son in the likeness of sinful flesh, on account of sin: He condemned sin in the flesh, that the righteous requirements of the law might be fulfilled in us who do not walk according to the flesh but according to the Spirit.

So then, those who are in the flesh cannot please God. But you are not in the flesh but in the Spirit, if indeed the Spirit of God dwells in you. Now if anyone does not have the Spirit of Christ, (the Christ Spirit) he is none of His. And if Christ is in you, the body is dead because of sin, but the Spirit is life because of righteousness.

But if the Spirit of Him who raised Jesus from the dead dwells in you, He who raised Christ from the dead will also give life to your mortal bodies through His Spirit who dwells in you" (Rm. 8:2-4, 8-11).

These last verses refer to the resurrection at the last day. However, looking at the first verses (2-4) and connecting the whole with verses (12-13) we can see that it applies also to the spiritual dynamic of the Christ resurrection life which now works in us. His glory is seen in us now as His resurrection life is being manifested in us through the Holy Spirit. As we, through the Spirit, put to death the deeds of the body we live His Holy Life.

This is what Paul the apostle was saying to Peter and the others who were leaning on the law for strength (which was weak through the flesh) as recorded in Galatians 2:11-21,

"Now when Peter had come to Antioch, I withstood him to his face because he was to be blamed; for before certain men came from James, he would eat with the Gentiles; but when they came, he withdrew and separated himself, fearing those who were of the circumcision.

And the rest of the Jews also played the hypocrite with him, so that even Barnabas was carried away with their hypocrisy.

But when I saw that they were not straightforward about the truth of the gospel, I said to Peter before them all, 'If you, being a Jew, live in the manner of Gentiles and not as the Jews, why do you compel Gentiles to live as Jews?

We who are Jews by nature, and not sinners of the Gentiles, knowing that a man is not justified by the works of the law but by faith in Jesus Christ, even we have believed in Jesus Christ, that we might be justified by faith in Christ and not by the works of the law; for by the works of the law no flesh shall be justified.

For I through the law died to the law that I might live to God. I have been crucified with Christ; it is no longer I who live, but Christ lives in me; and the life which I now live in the flesh I live by faith in the Son of God, who loved me and gave Himself for me.

I do not set aside the grace of God; for if righteousness comes through the law, then Christ died in vain."

This passage has been quoted in its entirety because it reveals the serious nature of this matter and the subtle difference between living by grace by the power of the inward life of the Spirit of Christ and living by the law by self effort. So insidious was this matter that even Peter and Barnabas (along with others) were led astray. But Paul (who had full revelation of this matter) confronted Peter, explaining it cannot be a mixture of the two. If righteousness comes by law (self effort) then Christ died for nothing. Grace is set aside (Gal. 2:21). On the contrary, he said that he was crucified with Christ (vicariously). "For I through the law died to the law that I might live to God" (Gal. 2:19). "It is no longer I who live, but Christ lives in me" (Gal.:20).

Those who receive Christ receive His glorious life.

"But to as many as did receive and welcome Him, He gave the authority (power, privilege right) to become the children of God, that is, to those who believe in – adhere to, trust in and rely on – His name; Who owe their birth neither to bloods, nor to the will of the flesh (that of physical impulse), nor to the will of man (that of a natural father), but to God, - They are born of God" (Jn. 1:12, 13 Amp).

Just as being born of Adam gave us natural life; so being born of God gives us God's spiritual life. Now the believer has natural life (*psuche*) in the flesh. And spirit life (*zoe*) in Christ.

These newborn babies, though precious in the Lord's sight, are not yet what God wants them to be. They are to "the praise of the glory of His grace" (Eph. 1:6), but are more likely to seek glory for themselves than to bring Him glory.

Take, for instance, a new believer who is talented, personable, intellectual, quick witted and physically attractive, etc. These natural qualities and abilities make this person a natural leader. If this person becomes involved in the church, he will likely be quickly elevated to position of leadership. He receives many compliments and much praise. He is more likely to be hindered than helped in spiritual development.

He may achieve success in gathering a large following but spiritual fruit will be non existent. He ministers out of his soul life to the souls of others. The spirit life of Jesus has difficulty coming forth.

In order for the Christ life to come forth, there must be a transformation. Transformation comes through the renewing of the mind. Renewing of the mind begins with a presenting of the bodies as living sacrifice, totally given to God (Holy) (Rm. 12:1-4). This experience can rightly be called "bearing your cross." The cross is where the will is surrendered to another. The surrendered living sacrifice proves by experience what is the good, acceptable and perfect will of the Lord.

The apostle Paul refers to his own life experience to illustrate this process. The result of his brokenness was an unequalled zeal to preach the gospel of Christ with very little concern for his own personal comfort and safety. He wrote, "For I am the least of the apostles, who am not worthy to be called an apostle, because I persecuted the church of God. But by the grace of God I am what I am, and His grace toward me was not in vain; but I laboured more abundantly than they all, yet not I, but the grace of God which was with me" (1 Cor. 15:9, 10).

Paul further describes his life of submissive service in his second letter to the Corinthians.

"For we do not preach ourselves, but Christ Jesus the Lord, and ourselves your bondservants for Jesus' sake. For it is the God who commanded light to shine out of darkness, who has shone in our hearts to give the light of the knowledge of the glory of God in the face of Jesus Christ. But we have this treasure in earthen vessels, that the excellence of the power may be of God and not of us. We are hard-pressed on every side, yet not crushed; we are perplexed, but not in despair; persecuted, but not forsaken; struck down, but not destroyed—always carrying about in the body the dying of the Lord Jesus, that the life of Jesus also may be manifested in our body. For we who live are always delivered to death for Jesus' sake, that the life of Jesus also may be manifested in our mortal flesh. So then death is working in us, but life in you" (2 Cor 4:5-12).

The same apostle speaks of being given a thorn in the flesh to buffet him.

"It is doubtless not profitable for me to boast. I will come to visions and revelations of the Lord: I know a man in Christ who fourteen years ago—whether in the body I do not know, or whether out of the body I do not know, God knows—such a one was caught up to the third heaven. And I know such a man — whether in the body or out of the body I do not know, God knows—how he was caught up into Paradise and heard inexpressible words, which it is not lawful for a man to utter. Of such a one I will boast; yet of myself I will not boast, except in my infirmities. For though I might desire to boast, I will not be a fool; for I will speak the truth. But I refrain, lest anyone should think of me above what he sees me to be or hears from me. And lest I should be exalted above measure by the abundance of the revelations, a thorn in the flesh was given to me, a messenger of Satan to buffet me, lest I be exalted above measure. Concerning this thing I pleaded with the Lord three times that it might depart from me. And He said to me, "My grace is sufficient for you, for My strength is made perfect in weakness." Therefore most gladly I will rather boast in my infirmities, that the power of

Christ may rest upon me. Therefore I take pleasure in infirmities, in reproaches, in needs, in persecutions, in distresses, for Christ's sake. For when I am weak, then I am strong" (2 Cor. 12:1-10).

The buffeting, meant by Satan to bring hurt, is allowed by the Lord to keep him from being "exalted above measure." It also brought him to see where true strength is found – not in self, but in the Lord. When Paul sought relief from the "thorn in the flesh," he was told by the Lord "My grace is sufficient for you" (verse 9). It seems the Lord was saying to Paul (and to us) "My grace is all you need." When he Lord explained that Paul's weakness (rather than his strength) gave the Lord's strength opportunity to work through him, Paul responded in essence, "If that's the way things work, then let me be weak. Let me gladly receive my limitations that Christ's greater power may rest upon me."

That is the attitude to which all thc sons must come in order that the glorious life of Christ can come through. The more the soul life is relied upon, the more the Christ life is limited and the more self is glorified.

What does this glory to which we are called look like? What form does it take? The full answer to this question will have to await the revealing of the sons of God, however, since "we shall be like Him" when He appears (1 Jn. 3:2), we can surmise it will be like the glory they "beheld" in Him when the "Word was made flesh, and dwelt among us (and we beheld His glory, the glory as of the only begotten of the Father) full of grace and truth" (Jn. 1:14 KJV).

The glory which they beheld was grace and truth. That is the same glory which was shown to Moses on the mountain when he asked the Lord to, "Please, show me your glory" (Ex. 33:18). The Lord answered Moses, "I will make all my goodness pass before you and — I will be gracious, — and I will have compassion" (Ex. 33:19). We read also "The Lord descended in the cloud and stood with him there, and proclaimed the name of the LORD. And the LORD passed before him and proclaimed 'The LORD, the LORD God, merciful and gracious, longsuffering, and abounding in goodness and truth, keeping mercy for thousands, forgiving iniquity and transgression and sin..." (Ex. 34:5-7).

God's glory is seen, not only in His shining (*shekinah*) but also in His character. Jesus was just like the Father. While on earth there was only one brief moment when His *shekinah* broke forth (on the mount of transfiguration) but the other aspect of God's glory (His character) could be seen all the time. His glory could be seen all the time. His glory could also be seen in His works. The glory of God was manifested as Jesus "went about doing good and healing all who were oppressed of the devil, for God was with Him" (Acts 10:38).

The sons, as "joint heirs with Christ" (Rm. 8:17) share in this glory. The more His life comes through, the more of His glory is seen.

To sum up then: God is bringing sons to His glory (Heb. 2:10). Since Christ and His brethren are all of One, He is not ashamed to call them "brethren" (Heb. 2:11). As joint heirs with Christ the brethren are called to suffer with Him that we might be glorified together with Him (Rm. 8:17). These sufferings are not worthy to be compared with the glory that shall be revealed in us (Rm. 8:18). There is to be a glorious appearing of our great God and Saviour Jesus Christ (Titus 2:13). When He appears we will appear with Him in glory. "For you died, and your life is hidden with Christ in God. When Christ who is our life appears, then you also will appear with Him in glory" (Col. 3:3, 4). And we shall be "like Him, for we shall see Him as He is" (1 Jn. 3:1, 2).

Let this serve as a rebuttal to those who teach the false doctrine that everyone and everything will eventually be restored. Only those who are "in Christ" will be His at His coming (1 Cor. 15:20-23). Just as all who are in Adam die, (that is every human being), so all who are in Christ shall be made alive. All others remain dead, awaiting judgment. (See Jn.5:24-3; Rev. 20:11-15)

Chapter Two

We See Not Yet

To say that man is a very special created being is almost an understatement. To recognize that man was created to have dominion is only part of the picture.

Man was created in God's very image and likeness. He is in the God class of being. No other is in that class. Man is not equal to God, but he is the same type of being. Attributes of God cannot be ascribed to man but His likeness can.

Man's destiny is to have dominion over the works of God's hands, but his purpose for being is to fellowship with God. Being in fellowship with God is what qualifies man to rule over the works of God's hands.

Angels, though spirit beings, were not created for fellowship with God. They are servants who do His bidding but nowhere are we told the angels fellowship with God.

Therefore, they do not have dominion over the works of His hands. It is true some angels have positions of rule (archs) over other angels but that is the extent of their rule – over the angels assigned to them to accomplish God's will in that area.

Man, on the other hand, is destined to have dominion over all the works of God's hands (including angels). According to Hebrews 2:8 "He put all in subjection under him, He left nothing that is not put under him." Man, in fellowship with God has great significance.

What do we mean by "fellowship"? What does it mean that man may fellowship with God? Since the English word "fellowship" has come to mean little more than sitting and talking together or sharing a cup of coffee etc., perhaps we should use a different word when speaking of what happens between God and man or, for that matter, the deeper sharing between man and man. The word fellowship does carry the meaning of "sharing" (as in eating together or in communicating real feelings and words) but to express what is meant in Bible terminology we may need to use a different word in today's English.

First John 1:3 says, "that which we have seen and heard we declare to you, that you also may have fellowship with us; and truly our fellowship is with the Father and with His Son Jesus Christ."

The Greek word translated "fellowship" is *kononia*. The same word is used in 2 Corinthians 13:14 where it is translated "communion", where Paul speaks of the "communion of the Holy Spirit".

The meaning of the word includes; partnership, sharing together, giving and receiving, participation, social intercourse. The Philippians were commended by the apostle Paul in that they had "shared" (*Gr. sugkoinoneo*) with (him) in (his) distress (Phil 4:14) and also they had "shared" (*Gr. kononeo*) in giving and receiving (Phil. 4:15).

Why am I stressing this so strongly? To establish the point that man, of necessity, must be in the God class of being since he can fellowship with God. None of His other created beings (as far as I know) can fellowship with God. They can communicate with Him and He with them, but that is only one aspect of fellowship. The angels "bless the Lord", they "hearken to the voice of His word and they are His ministers who do His pleasure" (Ps. 103:20), but they are not in the God class of Beings and, therefore, do not fellowship with Him. (Otherwise, why would He create man in His image and likeness?)

As long as man remained in fellowship with God he maintained dominion over the works of God's hands as specified. When fellowship was broken through his disobedience, man was no longer in the position of "lord" over the earth. Although the position was usurped by Satan, it is not his to keep. It is to be restored to man. Even though man, (in his fallen state) is unable to function in the role of governor, the position is reserved for him. The Man Of God, Christ Jesus has redeemed it and it will be completely restored at His return.

The "headquarters" from which man was to govern things on earth was the garden where he had uninterrupted communion with God. Fellowship was essential for man to fulfill his role because he was God's "partner". He was God's representative to do things God wanted done. When man fell into a self-centered, self-motivating mode, he was removed from headquarters (the Garden of Eden).

Imagine what earth would be like forever if God left matters exclusively in man's selfish control. "The earth is the Lord's" (Ps. 24:1). God has not forsaken it. He is watching over it to bring it into His expected purpose.

Satan is called "the god of this world" (2 Cor. 4:4), not of the earth. He is referred to as the "prince of the power of the air" but not Prince of earth. He has a stolen place of influence over fallen man, who "walks according to this spirit who now works in the children of disobedience" (Eph. 2:2), but this is not a permanent condition.

God's eternal, infallible purpose still stands. His plan involves the redemption of man and of nature. The price of redemption has already been paid and the power of the resurrection is at work in the lives of those who have believed on the Lord. The redemption will be completed at the coming of the Lord in the glory of His kingdom and when resurrection is complete.

Some teach that we are in the kingdom now. I would say we are in the kingdom now but not in the kingdom age which is not yet come on earth. "He has delivered us from the power of darkness and conveyed us into the kingdom of the Son of His love" (Col. 1:13). We also read, "I charge you therefore before God and the Lord Jesus Christ, who will judge the living and the dead at His appearing and His kingdom" (2 Tim. 4:1). This indicates there is some aspect in which His kingdom has not yet come.

Others teach that, now that we are in the kingdom, and God has made us kings and priests, (Rev. 1:6, 5:10) we are to reign here and now. We are to have the best of everything, control the elements, manipulate the animals, control our own destiny etc. We are the head and not the tail, we can have whatever we want. Evidently, someone forgot to inform Paul the apostle of this. He wrote to his carnal minded children at Corinth, "For who makes you differ from another? And what do you have that you did not receive? Now if you indeed did receive it, why do you boast as if you had not received it?

You are already full! You are already rich! You have reigned as kings without us – and indeed I could wish you did reign, that we might reign with you" (1 Cor. 4:7, 8).

If we fail to catch he cynicism here, we miss the full impact of this passage. You may question the use of the word cynicism here seeing this is the Word of God. Neither God nor His servant Paul are cynics: "A faultfinding captious critic: one who believes that human conduct is motivated wholly by self interest" (Webster). Both; however, may make a cynical remark: "contemptuously distrustful of human nature and motives (Webster). I cannot think of a better word to express the tone of these verses. These were carnal minded believers who were pridefully puffed up because of the particular teacher they were attached to. They considered themselves full. They were rich, having access to all that God possessed. They called themselves kings and considered to be already reigning.

Paul is not complimenting these believers! This is not a word of encouragement to cheer them on in their pursuits. This becomes clear when Paul says to them, "I could wish you did reign, that we might reign with you" (1 Cor. 4:8). In fact, they are not now reigning.

There is coming a day when those who suffer with Christ now will reign with Him then (Rm. 8:17)! That day has not arrived, else Paul would be reigning with them.

But did not this same apostle write to the believers at Rome, "....they which receive abundance of grace and the gift of righteousness shall reign in life by one, Jesus Christ" (Rm. 5:17). Yes, he did, and the context makes clear what type of reigning he is referring to. Death reigned through sin over Adam and his posterity. Those who receive abundance of Grace and the gift of righteousness shall reign" (v. 17) over sin in life and righteousness.

"For if, because of one man's trespass (lapse, offense) death reigned through that one, much more surely will those who receive (God's) overflowing grace (unmerited favor) and the free gift of righteousness (putting them into right standing with Himself) reign as kings in life through the One, Jesus Christ, the Messiah, the Anointed One" (Rm. 5:17. Amp)

Revelation 1:5 and 4:10 does say that God made us kings and priests. "To Him who loved us and washed us from our sins in His own blood, and has made us kings and priests to His God and Father" (Rev. 1:5,6) "and made us kings and priests to our God; and we shall reign on earth". Does not this mean we reign as kings on earth now? Not necessarily.

Notice some things about these verses: In the first place we are said to be kings and priests unto His God and Father and to our God (not necessarily on earth). A cross reference immediately takes us to Exodus 19:6. Here we read "And you shall be to Me a kingdom of priests and a holy nation" (speaking of Israel). In a like sense we are now a kingdom of priests unto God after the order of Melchizedek. When Abraham met this king/priest he recognized him as priest of the most High God. He was a king but that is not mentioned here. He was the king of the city of Salem. He may be as much a king outside the city as he is inside but he has no authority here. When he returns to Salem he will be in full authority.

Jesus has been given all authority in heaven and on earth (Mt. 28:18). Because of that He has delegated us to act in

His Name, as His representatives. We act only in His Name, which means we do what He would do in that circumstance. He has made us kings and we shall reign on earth when He is seated on His throne in Jerusalem. "To him who overcomes will I grant to sit with Me in My throne, as I overcame and sat down with My Father on His throne" (Rev. 3:21). He is now seated with His Father on His throne. When He returns He will sit on His throne, the throne of His father David, on earth. Yes, we are kings now, but we wait until later to reign with Him.

Concerning earthly possessions the apostle has some strong words. His attitude toward his own financial status is expressed in his letter to the Philippians, "Not that I speak in regard to need, for I have learned in whatsoever state I am, to be content: I know how to be abased, and I know how to abound. Everywhere and in all things I have learned to be full and to be hungry, both to abound and to suffer need. I can do all things through Christ who strengthen me" (Phil. 4:11-13).

His attitude toward wealth itself is expressed in His letter to the Corinthians, "But this I say, brethren, the time is short, so that those who .... Buy as though they did not possess, and those who use this world as not misusing it. For the form of this world is passing away" (1 Cor. 7:29-31) and again, "as poor and making many rich; as having nothing and yet possessing all things" (2 Cor. 6:10).

As for those who are entrusted with the wealth of this world and those who seek it, he writes,

".... Useless wrangling of men of corrupt minds and destitute of the truth, who suppose that godliness is a means of gain. From such withdraw yourself. Now godliness with contentment is great gain.

For we brought nothing into this world, and it is certain we can carry nothing out. And having food and clothing, with these we shall be content. But those who desire to be rich fall into temptation and a snare, and into many foolish and harmful lusts which drawn men in destruction and perdition. For the love of money is the root of all kinds of evil, for which some have strayed from the faith in their greediness, and pierced themselves through with many sorrows.

But you O Man of God, flee these things and pursue righteousness, godliness, faith, love, patience, gentleness. Fight the good fight of faith, lay hold on eternal life, to which you were also called..." (1 Tim. 6:5-12).

"Command those who are rich in this present age not to be haughty, nor to trust in uncertain riches but in the living God, who gives us richly all things to enjoy" (1 Tim. 6:17). For those who covet the wealth of others and try to justify it with Proverbs 13:22, "..... the wealth of the sinners is stored up for the righteous", I would urge that they look at the entire verse and check Psalm 49 for God's commentary on this subject. The entire verse is, "A good man leaves an inheritance to his children's children. But the wealth of the sinner is stored up for the righteous". When do the grandchildren receive their inheritance? Is it not when the grandfather is gone? In the same way the wealth of sinners will accrue to the account of the righteous when he is gone. The sinner can take nothing away, so it is left here for the meek when they inherit the earth.

Psalm 49:10 gives the correct sense, "For he sees wise men die; Likewise the fool and the senseless person perish, and leave their wealth to others". (Please read all of Psalm 49 for God's commentary on this matter.)

The Corinthians were not now reigning, living a life of luxury, and neither was Paul. He gives us a glimpse of his own life experience. His was not a life of ease spent in a beautiful mansion with three golden chariots in the garage and thirty-six white horses in the stalls.

"For I think that God has displayed us, the apostles, last, as men condemned to death; for we have been made a spectacle to the world, both to angels and to men.

We are fools for Christ's sake, but you are wise in Christ! We are weak but you are strong! You are distinguished, but we are dishonored! (See the cynicism again.) To this present hour we both hunger and thirst, and we are poorly clothed, and beaten, and homeless. And we labor, working with our own hands" (1 Cor. 4:9).

Paul refused to impose himself on others. There is no record of him receiving a love offering for himself. He received offerings for the poor in Jerusalem, worked with his own hands to provide for himself and those who were with him. He was content with whatever was provided for him.

Then he asked others to imitate him. This, of course requires denying self and taking up our cross.

This is in sharp contrast to today's American ministers who consider success to be wearing expensive clothes, drive fancy cars and live in big houses. Paul's main concern was to protect the integrity of the ministry and bring glory to God.

"We give no offense in anything, that our ministry may not be blamed. But in all things we commend ourselves as ministers of God: in much patience, in tribulations, in needs, in distresses, in stripes, in imprisonments, in tumults, in labors, in sleeplessness, in fastings; by purity, by knowledge, by long-suffering, by kindness, by the Holy Spirit, by sincere love, by the word of truth, by the power of God, by the armor of righteousness on the right hand and on the left, by honor and dishonor, by evil report and good report; as deceivers, and yet true; as unknown and yet well known; as dying, and behold we live; as chastened, and yet not killed; as sorrowful, yet always rejoicing; as poor, yet making many rich; as having nothing, and yet possessing all things" (2 Cor. 6:3-10).

This lengthy excursion just to say, "Yes, but not yet".

The letter to the Hebrews quotes from the eighth Psalms, "For He has not put the world to come, of which we speak, in subjection to angels, saying, 'What is man that you are mindful of him, or the son of man that you take care of him? You have made him little lower than the angels; you have crowned him with glory and honor; and set him over the works of your hands. You have put all things in subjection under his feet'. For in that he put all in subjection under him, He left nothing that is not put under him. But now we see not yet all things put under him" (Heb. 2:5-8).

We note here that man is intended to rule over the works of God's hands. Man's fall into sin (and out of fellowship with God) only temporarily (and not unexpectedly) interrupted the plan of God. It did not alter it.

We should note also that the designation is further explained. Not only is man's jurisdiction over sheep and oxen (domesticated animals), beasts of the field (undomesticated animals), birds and fish (Ps. 8:6-8), but "over all the works of Your hands. The word "all" in Psalm 8:6 is specifically explained as inclusive of everything such that "He left nothing that is not put under him". This would, of course not include God Himself.

"But now we see not yet all things put under him. But we see, Jesus – crowned with glory and honor" (Heb. 2:9). This man, Jesus was the man of God's intention from the beginning. (More on this in the next chapter.)

Why did God begin on earth with Adam? (I specify "on earth" because this did not begin on earth, but in eternity.) Adam is not God's Firstborn. He was the first man created by God, but Jesus is God's Firstborn. (See Chapter One) God's procedure on earth is, "First the natural, and then the spiritual" (1 Cor. 15:46). (This in no way means the natural was first in the mind and purpose of God. It is only a necessary stage in the realization of the finished product.) A limited illustration might be construction of a building. We might say that the natural beginning was procurement of lumber, nails, etc. The building began long before that. The building began in the mind of the architect. He began it (and in a sense finished it) in his mind before ever getting materials together.

In the natural it began when "the Lord God formed man of the dust of the ground, and breathed into his nostrils the breath of life; and man became a living being" (Gen. 2:7).

We have no way of knowing how long before this the Lord said, "Let us make man in our image, according to Our likeness". We do know that "He chose" us in Him (Christ) before the foundation of the world" (Eph. 1:4). So we were in the plan and purpose of God before the beginning of creation. It is clear, also, that Christ was the true Head from the beginning.

Why does Psalms Eight and Hebrews Two speak of "man" and "the son of man"? The son of man spoken of here is not primarily Jesus Christ who is the Son of Man. (See Dean Alford and others quoted by him in his New Testament For English Readers pg. 1457.) It seems to me, the Holy Spirit is here referring not to man the original creation but to the man recreated in Christ Jesus. Paul, in First Corinthians Fifteen discusses the nature of the resurrection. As natural men we are born into Adam (from his loins and therefore of his kind). The first man is of earth and related to earthly things. The second man is the Lord from heaven, related to things above (See 1 Cor. 15:45-49).

To illustrate the resurrection and "with what body do they come" (1 Cor. 15:35). Paul uses a grain of wheat. We place a grain of wheat in the ground, it dies and yet lives. God gives it a body as He pleases. The seed we bury in the ground is the same that sprouts up; but how different! So is the resurrection of our body. It is sown a natural body and raised a spiritual body. The old is not raised up and yet it is out of the death of the old the new comes. It is the seed of the woman which is resurrected. God created man male and female. It was through the male, sin entered the race. The female, though involved, was not the responsible "head". Through the Seed of the female, salvation has come. It is that seed which is raised to walk in newness of life.

"Therefore we were buried with Him through baptism into death, that just as Christ was raised from the dead by the glory of the Father, even so we also should walk in newness of life. For if we have been united together in the likeness of His death, certainly we shall be in the likeness of His resurrection" (Rm. 6:4,5).

So let us review a few things:

- There is a reason for man being created lower than angels. This is only stage one.
- The procedure is "first the natural then the spiritual" when dealing with man on earth.
- Jesus Christ is God's number One Son, not Adam.
- God intended from the beginning that Jesus Christ should reign.

Not only is Christ destined to sit on the throne of David to reign, those who overcome shall also reign with Him. "To him who overcomes I will grant to sit with Me on My throne, as I also overcame and sat down with My Father on

His throne" (Rev. 3:21). Both they and He will be in resurrection bodies. So that is yet future.

Meanwhile, in this present life, believers are being equipped and conditioned to reign with him.

"For as many as are being constantly led by God's Spirit, these are sons of God. For you did not receive a spirit of slavery again with resulting fear, but you received the Spirit who places you as adult sons, by whom we cry out with deep emotion, Abba, |namely| Father. The Spirit himself is constantly bearing joint-testimony with our |human| spirit that we are God's children and since children, also heirs; on the one hand, heirs of God, on the other, joint-heirs with Christ, provided that we are suffering with Him in order that we also may be glorified together, for I have come to a reasoned conclusion that the sufferings of the present season are of no weight in comparison to the glory which is about to be revealed upon us.

For the concentrated and undivided expectation of the creation is assiduously and patiently awaiting the revelation of the sons of God; for the creation was subjected to futility, not voluntarily but on account of the One who put it under subjection upon the basis of the hope that the creation itself also will be delivered from the bondage of corruption into the liberty of the glory of the children of God. For we know that the whole creation groans and travails together up to this moment, and not only, but we ourselves also who have the first-fruit of the Spirit, we ourselves also are groaning within ourselves, assiduously and patiently waiting the full realization of our adult sonship at the time of the redemption of our body. For we were saved in the sphere of hope. But hope that has been seen is not hope, for that which a person sees, why does he hope for it? But if that which we do not see, we hope for, through patience we expectantly wait for it.

And in like manner also the Spirit lends us a helping hand with reference to our weakness, for the particular thing that we should pray for according to what is necessary in the nature of the case, we do not know with an absolute knowledge; but the Spirit himself comes to our rescue by interceding with unutterable groanings. Moreover, He who is constantly searching our hearts knows what is the mind of the Spirit because, according to God, He continually makes intercession on behalf of the saints.

And we know with an absolute knowledge that for those who are loving God, all things are working together resulting in good for those who are divinely-summoned ones according to His purpose. Because, those whom He foreordained He also marked out beforehand as those who were to be conformed to the derived image of His Son, with the result that He is firstborn among many brethren. Moreover, those whom He thus marked out beforehand, these He also summoned. And those whom He summoned, these He also justified. Moreover, those whom He justified, these He also glorified" (Rm. 8:14-30 Kenneth S. Wuest Expanded Translation).

Equipping and developing the saints involves going through difficulties and opposition. We are to be encouraged as we face all kinds of opposition, ridicule, rejection, deprivations, trials and tribulations, knowing that all these "light affliction, which is but for a moment, is working for us a far more exceeding and eternal weight of glory" (2 Cor. 4:17). We must "be steadfast, immovable, always abounding in the work of the Lord, knowing that (our) labor is not in vain in the Lord" (1 Cor. 15:58).

We walk by faith, not by sight (2 Cor. 5:7) while we "look not at the things which are seen, but at things not seen. For the things which are seen are temporal, but the things which are not seen are eternal" (2 Cor. 4:18).

"Therefore do not cast away your confidence, which has great reward. For you have need of endurance, so that after you have done the will of God, you may receive the promise: For yet a little while, and He who is coming will come and will not tarry. Now the just shall live by faith...." (Heb. 10:35-37).

Since then we were raised with Christ (Eph. 2:4,5), we are to "seek those things which are above, where Christ is, sitting at the right hand of God". We are to "set (our) affection on things above, not on things on the earth. For (we) died, and (our) life is hidden with Christ in God. When Christ who is our life appears (*Gr. phaino "shine"*) then you also shall appear (*Gr. phaino "shine"*) with Him in glory" (Col. 3:3,4).

Chapter Three

But We See Jesus Crowned

"For He has not put the world to come, of which we speak, in subjection to angels. But one testified in a certain place, saying: "What is man that You are mindful of him, Or the son of man that You take care of him? You have made him a little lower than the angels; You have crowned him with glory and honor, And set him over the works of Your hands. You have put all things in subjection under his feet." For in that He put all in subjection under him, He left nothing that is not put under him. But now we do not yet see all things put under him. But we see Jesus, who was made a little lower than the angels, for the suffering of death crowned with glory and honor, that He, by the grace of God, might taste death for everyone. For it was fitting for Him, for whom are all things and by whom are all things, in bringing many sons to glory, to make the captain of their salvation perfect through sufferings. For both He who sanctifies and those who are being sanctified are all of one, for which reason He is not ashamed to call them brethren..." (Hebrews 2:5-11)

L et me state again my complete astonishment at the fact that He who for whom and by whom all things were created became man. My mind is overwhelmed at the very thought that He could create this great universe (of which we learn more every day) could also become man, and yet this is clearly taught in the scriptures.

Another wonderful awe inspiring discovery is that this was not an after thought or emergency recovery arrangement on the part of God. It is what He had planned and purposed from the very beginning. As before stated God did not plan Adam to fail but He did plan for Jesus to succeed.

It is in the Epistle to the Hebrews we learn that when the eight Psalms referred to man being made "little lower than angels" it referred to status as well as time, and that it also included Jesus Christ.

Adam was made lower than the angels but would eventually be over the works of God's hands (See Chapter Two). It was necessary for man to be in the natural state first. This was the beginning of the process by which came the union of God with man (See Chapter Two).

Jesus Christ was also made lower than angels for a short while (and for a specific purpose). The First Begotten Son, in the state of "being in the form of God" (Phil. 2:6) could not die. (How could God die?) So He laid aside whatever was necessary for Him to become man (though He never ceased to be God), that He might identify with man to the extent He could take man's sin and die in his place.

> "But we see Jesus, who was made a little lower than the angels, for the suffering of death ....that He, by the grace of God, might taste death for everyone."

In this sense Jesus has become our "Kinsman Redeemer". To be Kinsman Redeemer He must become one with His brethren, "For both He who sanctifies and they who are being sanctified are all of one, for which reason He is not ashamed to call them brethren" (Heb. 2:11). (See Chapter Five for more about the kinsman redeemer.)

Having become flesh and blood man He must be perfected as their captain.

"For it was fitting for Him, for whom are all things and by whom are all things, in bringing many sons to glory, to make the captain (author, originator) of their salvation perfect (complete) through sufferings" (Heb. 2:10).

Jesus was a perfect man, but He was not a perfect Saviour until He had completed the work which the Father had given Him to do.

"Though He was a son, yet learned He obedience by the things which He suffered. And having been perfected, He became the author of eternal salvation to all who obey Him" (Heb. 5:8,9).

The word translated "perfected" can also mean "completeness". Until Jesus became our sin offering and was sacrificed for us, our salvation was not completed. Once the judgment for sin was satisfied Jesus was resurrected because we were now justified.

"....(righteousness) shall be imputed to us who believe in Him who raised up Jesus our Lord from the dead, who was delivered up because of our offenses, and was raised because of our justification" (Rm. 4:24,25).

Jesus perfected (finished) the work the Father had given Him to do. He obeyed His Father perfectly throughout His entire life. He learned obedience through the things He suffered. What does it mean "He learned obedience"? It does not say He learned to obey. He had always obeyed. He would have had to learn to disobey. Jesus learned obedience when He was faced with the choices of His will or His Father's will. At that point, through intense prayers, supplications, vehement cries and tears, He submitted Himself to the Father's will. Jesus would have chosen not to drink the cup had it not been the Father's will to drink it.

We might do well to ponder that cup which troubled Jesus so. Surely it was not his physical death on the cross, no matter how cruel and hideous. He had known for weeks that He was going to Jerusalem to die on the cross. He had attempted to tell His followers about it. He had "set His face" to go to Jerusalem as though looking forward to finishing His work on earth.

It seems as though the content of the cup is what disturbed Him so. Is it possible that when He, the altogether pure, holy Son of God/Son of Man, saw the fullness of what was in that cup His Holy Being recoiled in horror? The composite of the total filth of the human race; which He was asked to drink to the bottom, made Him quake with dread. Knowing that His Holy Father could not continue the unbroken fellowship with His Son until He had paid the debt in full, and that only then could He raise Him up through the Spirit of Holiness, into eternal fellowship, He was in agony.

It was not just the physical pain of the horrible crucifixion, nor was it the shame of being made a public spectacle, it was the "making His soul an offering for sin" (Is. 53:10), the "(being made) to be sin for us" (2 Cor. 5:21) that caused Him such grief. For now He appears before His Holy Father and the holy angels as our sin. Now that He is before the Just Judge as our sin, the full wrath of Holy God against unrighteousness is poured out upon Him until the "holy, just and good law" (Rm. 7:12) is perfectly satisfied. The agony of the decision to become our sin was such that He sweat great drops of blood and might have perished here in Gethsemane had not an angel strengthened Him so His tortured soul and weakened body could proceed through this torment to the physical torture and pain of the nails to die on the tree as a curse for us.

When Jesus looked into the "cup" and saw the full depths of degradation which He was asked to take upon His holy person He recoiled and requested, "Father, "O my Father, if it be possible, let this cup pass from me: nevertheless not as I will, but as thou wilt".

There is not the slightest hint here of shrinking His responsibility, no indication of inclination to disobey, only resignation that the Father's will be done. Here He "learned" obedience when it is His will to remain holy and in fellowship with His Father but willing to "be made to be sin;" if that be the Father's will. Through what happened in Gethsemane, on cavalry, and in the tomb, Jesus has now become perfect salvation as far as justification is concerned. There remains one other aspect of being made perfect as our Saviour.

We need a High Priest to make the perfect sacrifice for us before Holy God. Jesus had to be tempted in all points as we are, go through every human experience men face, that He might be a merciful and faithful High Priest.

"Therefore, in all things He had to be made like His brethren, that He might be a merciful and faithful High Priest in things pertaining to God, to make propitiation for the sins of the people. For in that He Himself has suffered, being tempted, He is able to aid those who are tempted (Heb. 2:17, 18).

Hebrews 5:5-10 also speaks of the perfecting of Jesus as our High Priest: "So also Christ did not glorify Himself "to become High Priest, but it was He who said to Him: ' You are My Son, Today I have begotten You.' As He also says in another place: 'You are a priest forever according to the order of Melchizedek'; who, in the days of His flesh, when He had offered up prayers and supplications, 'with vehement cries and tears to Him who was able to save Him from death, and was heard because of His godly fear, though He was a Son, yet He learned obedience by the things which he suffered. And having been perfected, He became the author of eternal salvation to all who obey Him, called by God as High Priest 'according to the order of Melchizedek".

Though we do not yet see "all things" under the rulership of man, we do see The Man, Christ Jesus crowned with glory and honor. Jesus, in the Book of Revelation, indicated He is at this time seated with the Father on His throne (Rev. 3:21).

Paul tells us this is in His ministry as mediator between God and man.

"For there is one God, and one Mediator between God and man, the M<u>an</u> Christ Jesus" (1 Tim 2:5 emphasis on Man).

Jesus, as man is seated with God on His throne. So man, in the Headship of Christ, is already over the works of God's hands. Others who are qualified, will eventually be brought to this glory.

We can conclude this chapter with a few general observations. To do justice to the subject of this chapter would require a great volume. Our subject matter has to do more with bringing other sons to the glory which they will share with the First Begotten. Bringing that Son into the glory due His name will require eternity.

The process for bringing this Son into His glory serves as a pattern for all others who shall be brought into glory.

"Let nothing be done through selfish ambition or conceit, but in lowliness of mind let each esteem others better than himself. Let each of you look out not only for his own interests, but also for the interests of others. Let this mind be in you which was also in Christ Jesus, who, being in the form of God, did not consider it robbery to be equal with God, but made Himself of no reputation, taking the form of a bondservant, and coming in the likeness of men. And being found in appearance as a man, He humbled Himself and became obedient to the point of death, even the death of the cross. Therefore God also has highly exalted Him and given Him the name which is above every name, that at the name of Jesus every knee should bow, of those in heaven, and of those on earth, and of those under the earth, and that every tongue should confess that Jesus Christ is Lord, to the glory of God the Father" (Phil. 2:3-11).

In conclusion: Jesus is the God/Man ruling with God on His throne. He is the second man, the spiritual man. He is High Priest of the new order of man. He is Supreme Ruler over the works of God's hands. He has been given jurisdiction in heaven and on earth. He has been given the most excellent name. He has inherited the covenants God made with Abraham and his seed and David and his seed.

At this time He is waiting for the bride to be completed and prepared, a church without spot, wrinkle or any imperfection.

Chapter Four

Making Sons

"He was in the world, and the world was made through Him, and the world did not know Him. He came to His own, and His own did not receive Him. But as many as received Him, to them He gave the right to become children of God, to those who believe in His name: who were born, not of blood, nor of the will of the flesh, nor of the will of man, but of God" (Jn. 1:10-13).

The Father has one Son already in glory. He is the God/ Man, the Messiah. God's intent and purpose, however, was to bring many sons to glory. This was His purpose from the beginning. He has stretched forth His hand to accomplish His purpose and no one and no combination of forces can turn it back. The unparalleled privilege of being part of this divine destiny is extended to "whosoever will": but is limited to "those who receive Him, to those who believe in His name" (Jn. 1:12).

There is a necessary process through which these sons are brought to glory. We must come in at the narrow gate and proceed along the way which leads to life. "Because narrow is the gate and difficult is the way which leads to life, and there are few that find it" (Mt. 7:14).

Jesus said, "I am the way, the truth, and the life, no one comes to the Father except through Me" (Jn. 14:6). In Proverbs 14:12 we read, "There is a way that seems right to a man but its end is the way of death".

It seems to man if we just do our best, live a reasonably good life, try to keep the ten commandments, and treat other people right, God will be pleased with us. Surely He would welcome that kind of person into His kingdom. From the human standpoint that certainly seems right, but it is still the broad way referred to by Jesus. Most people, He said, are on this broad way that leads to destruction.

The problem with that type of thinking is that it is of man in his natural state of being. Jesus is not being narrow minded, nor is He trying to make it difficult for man to enter the kingdom of God. The natural state is one thing and the spiritual state is another. The kingdom of God is spiritual. Man, in the natural state (flesh and blood) cannot inherit the kingdom of God, corruption does not inherit incorruption (1 Cor. 15:50). In fact, the natural man cannot even understand the things of the spirit. "But the natural man does not receive the things of the Spirit of God, for they are foolishness to him; nor can he know them, because they are spiritually discerned" (1 Cor. 2:14).

That is what Jesus is explaining to Nicodemus (a ruler of the Jews) in John Chapter Three. Jesus said to this religious leader who was not only living by the law the best he could, but teaching the same to others, "Most assuredly, I say to you, unless one is born again, he cannot see the kingdom of God" (Jn. 3:3). Jesus went on to say, "Most assuredly, I say to you, unless one is born of water and of the Spirit, he cannot enter the kingdom of God. That which is born of the flesh is flesh, and that which is born of the Spirit is spirit" (Jn. 3:5, 6).

To enter into or understand the spiritual kingdom of God, we must be born again, born from above, born of the Spirit. This is not another physical birth into the natural, but a spiritual birth within. This begins the spiritual process of transformation that culminates in our being completely conformed into the spiritual image of Jesus Christ.

God made Adam of the dust of the earth, breathed into his nostrils the breath of life and he became a living soul (being) (Gen. 2:7). Adam was created of this earth, earthy. He was not created to fall but he was created fallible. All who are of Adam are like him. When Adam sinned, all sinned. When Christ died for Adam's sinful race, all died (vicariously) (2 Cor. 5:14).

When those of Adam's race, who are dead in trespasses and in sins, believe in the death of Christ on the cross as their sin offering, dying for their sin, and when they receive Him as their resurrected Lord and Savior, they become born of His Spirit. They are born again, not of corruptible seed (from Adam) but of the incorruptible (seed) through the word of God, which liveth and abides forever (1 Pet. 1:23). Whereas, before, they were dead in trespasses and sins, they are made alive with the life of God. They are born, not of the will of the flesh, but of God (Jn. 1:12).

These newborn (spiritual) babes, are part of God's new creation in Christ. They have been given a new heart, they are alive toward God; Christ is now their Head. They are under a new covenant where their sins are remembered no more (Heb. 8:8-12).

As new born babes they need the milk of the word that they may grow thereby (1 Pet. 2:2). These are mere spiritual infants and must be given gentle care that they may reach spiritual maturity. To leave these spiritual babes to fend for themselves would be more tragic than neglecting natural newborns.

God will not leave these who are His children orphans. Jesus promised, "If you love me, keep my commandments. And I will pray the Father, and He will give you another Helper, that He may abide with you forever – The Spirit of truth, whom the world cannot receive, because it neither sees Him nor knows Him; but you know Him, for He dwells with you and will be in you. I will not leave you orphans; I will come to you" (Jn. 14:15-18).

These little ones have the Spirit of truth living within to help them grow. The word (the milk and later the meat) which He gives us is the word of truth about Christ. Jesus said, "However, when He, the Spirit of truth, has come, He will guide you into all truth; for He will not speak on His own authority but whatever He hears, He will speak; and He will tell you things to come.

He will glorify me, for He will take of what is Mine and declare it to you" (Jn. 16:13-14).

What happens when the Holy Spirit shows us the things of Christ is truly wonderful. The things of Christ which the Holy Spirit declares to us is what Jesus was like in life while here on earth and that His life is the same in us now. He is the same yesterday, today, and forever (Heb. 13:8). He is the same now as He was in the past. He is the same now as in the future. He is the same on earth as in heaven. His life is the same in us as it is in Him. The Holy Spirit shows us Christ. While we "with unveiled face, (behold) as in a mirror the glory of the Lord, (we) are being transformed into the same image from glory to glory, just as by the Spirit of the Lord" (2 Cor. 3:18).

Another provision the Lord has provided for our development in spirit are the gifts of Christ in the person of men who are gifted in such a way as to help develop (equip) us. These men are extensions of Christ Himself in His ministry to His church. They are called, "apostles, prophets, evangelists, pastors and teachers". They are given grace according to the measure of Christ's gift (Eph. 4:7) for the specific work of "equipping the saints for the ministry, for the edifying (building up) of the body of Christ, till we all come to the unity of the faith and of the knowledge of the Son of

God, to a perfect man, to the measure of the stature of the fullness of Christ" (See Eph. 4:10-16).

Every member of the body of Christ is to be involved in ministry. The work of the gifted gifts (men mentioned above) is to assist each member to discover his and her gifting that the members, speaking the truth in love, may grow up in all things into Him who is the head – Christ - from whom the whole body, joined and knit together by what every joint supplies, according to the effective working by which every part does its share, causes growth of the body for the edifying of itself in love" (Eph. 4:7, 11-16).

This is very critical. Babies do not grow into maturity by taking only milk. Healthy people grow by feeding, exercising, learning about themselves, relating to others, learning how to walk, talk, work, etc. It is the same in our spiritual life. Healthy spiritual lives grow into maturity.

Normal, healthy spiritual lives grow as we learn who we are in Christ and what He is in us. It is essential that we discover the difference between the soul led life and the Spirit led life. The soul life (self) is not evil when it is functioning according to God's design for it. It becomes evil when it is out of God's order.

God created man a living being (soul). He was a rea-soning, emotional, volitional being. None of these are evil in and of themselves, as long as they function within the param-eters established by the Creator. Man could also commune with the Creator through the spiritual faculty which came through the breath *(Heb. ruwach – spirit, to make of quick understanding)* which came from God. This higher faculty (life) was the means by which man could communicate with God. This kept the man submissive and obedient to God, as long as the soul life (reasoning, choices, and emotional feel-ings) were kept under the spirit. When man thought other than what God gave him to know, desired that which would please himself rather than God, and chose to partake of what God had specifically commanded him not to eat, he became self taught (knowing good and evil), self pleasing (took that which was good for food outside the provisions of God) and self determining (became as god).

When man is "born again" – (of the Spirit) he is able once again to commune with God, "we receive the spirit of adop-tion by whom we cry out Abba Father" (Rm. 8:15). To mature spiritually the believer must come to realize the self-centered life is detrimental to spiritual development and, therefore, must be denied. He must take up his cross and follow Christ.

We must choose the Spirit life over the soul life. In the words of the apostle, Paul, "For I through the law died to the law that I might live to God. I have been crucified with Christ; it is no longer I who live, but Christ lives in me; and the life I now live in the flesh I live by faith in the Son of God, who loved me and gave Himself for me" (Gal. 2:19,20).

For maximum efficiency in the process of bringing sons to glory (which involves maturing the saints), the church needs the right message and the correct structure. The message must be designed to feed the flock at every stage of development. The structure needs to be such that every member of the body of Christ is involved in the work of ministry.

Here are some questions to ponder: Was the message of the church in its beginning a timeless message? Is it as applicable to the real needs of modern man as it was to those of the first century of the church? Do we need to modernize the message to make it current? If preachers can simplify the Bible so that anyone who reads it can understand it, why do we need the Holy Spirit to illumine it? Why did not the all wise God not make it simple in the first place?

Maybe we need to reconsider the nature of the Bible. Paul tells us the nature of the Scripture, how they came to be and how they are to be understood:

"And my speech and my preaching were not with persuasive words of human wisdom, but in demonstration of the Spirit and of power, that your faith should not be in the wisdom of men but in the power of God. However, we speak wisdom among those who are mature, yet not the wisdom of this age, nor of the rulers of this age, who are coming to nothing. But we speak the wisdom of God in a mystery, the hidden wisdom which God ordained before the ages for our glory, which none of the rulers of this age knew; for had they known, they would not have crucified the Lord of glory. But as it is written: "Eye has not seen, nor ear heard, nor have entered into the heart of man the things which God has prepared for those who love Him." But God has revealed them to us through His Spirit. For the Spirit searches all things, yes, the deep things of God. For what man knows the things of a man except the spirit of the man which is in him? Even so no one knows the things of God except the Spirit of God. Now we have received, not the spirit of the world, but the Spirit who is from God, that we might know the things that have been freely given to us by God. These things we also speak, not in words which man's wisdom teaches but which the Holy Spirit teaches, comparing spiritual things with spiritual. But the natural man does not receive the things of the Spirit of God, for they are foolishness to him; nor can he know them, because they are spiritually discerned" (1 Cor. 2:4-14).

The Holy Spirit inspires the speaker as he speaks and He also illumines the hearer to hear. He makes the application according to the real need of the hearer. The Bible is a spiritual book to edify us spiritually. Problems are solved from the inside out. It is not merely a book of principles which we apply to our situation. It is the voice of our Heavenly Father helping us to see that He is Himself our all sufficiency. He wants us to "Trust in the Lord with all (our) heart, and lean not on (our) own understanding" (Pr. 3:5).

To grow into spiritual maturity is to be conformed more and more to the Christ life within. If the preacher/teacher give us how to lessons (even from the Bible), we are still (and more and more) inclined to do it ourselves. Maturity in the natural is to become less and less dependant upon others and more and more self sufficient. Spiritual maturity is exactly the opposite. We become more dependent upon

Christ and His body, the church. We need "that which every joint supplies" (Eph. 4:16).

For this very reason we need to return to the structure of the church as Jesus structured it at the beginning. When we look at the church as it was in the Book of Acts it may appear to have very little organizational structure at all. Upon closer observation we see the ingenuity of the Holy Spirit' working. The church was not established as an organization (such as a social club or a business), but as an organism. An organization can function without being alive. If certain order is set up and each part performs its function, the organization can operate efficiently and produce the desired product. Not so with an organism. The organism is inherently dependent upon the driving force of its life. The life of the organism is what determines its nature. Its purpose is to live, and in living perform its purpose When the life goes out of an organism it ceases to operate.

The church, the body of Christ is an organism, totally dependent upon the Spirit of Life in Christ Jesus. Its purpose is eternal because its life source is eternal. The function of the body of Christ on earth is to demonstrate His life in word and in deed as members are brought to the maturity of the fullness of Christ.

The modern church (or what is called church) is far from the original structure. It is more a business than a body, an organization more than an organism. The present pastor CEO led structural organization of the church produces many church members, but few sons.

Our natural bodies grow to full stature through eating the right foods and getting the right kind of exercise. It is the same with the body of Christ. The next two chapters will discuss how Christ designed the structure of the church to provide every member opportunity for spiritual exercise and also the right kinds of spiritual food.

The evidence of spiritual maturity is unity within the body of Christ. Just as division is evidence of immaturity, so unity is evidence of maturity.

"And I, brethren, could not speak to you as to spiritual people but as to carnal, as to babes in Christ. I fed you with milk and not with solid food; for until now you were not able to receive it, and even now you are still not able; for where there are envy, strife, and divisions among you, are you not carnal and behaving like mere man? For when one says, "I am of Paul", and another, "I am of Apollo's", are you not carnal" (1 Cor. 3:1-4).

Today's parallel to that would be following the particular teaching of some individual or group while rejecting truth taught by others. Overemphasis on some truths while rejecting other truth leads to sectarianism and even cults. There is only one body of Christ, but many members. We are then, partakers one with another.

Unity already exists in the spirit. Spiritual maturity is the result of coming into the unity of the faith and of the knowledge of the Son of God.

"Endeavoring to keep the unity of the Spirit in the bond of peace. *There is* one body and one Spirit, just as you were called in one hope of your calling; one Lord, one faith, one baptism; [6] one God and Father of all, who *is* above all, and through all, and in you all" (Eph. 4:3-6) and "till we all come to the unity of the faith and of the knowledge of the Son of God, to a perfect man, to the measure of the stature of the fullness of Christ; that we should no longer be children, tossed to and fro and carried about with every wind of doctrine, by the trickery of men, in the cunning craftiness of deceitful plotting, but, speaking the truth in love, may grow up in all things into Him who is the head—Christ— from whom the whole body, joined and knit together by what every joint supplies, according to the effective working by which every part does its share, causes growth of the body for the edifying of itself in love" (Eph. 4:13-36).

Another evidence of spiritual maturity is being able to receive deeper, heavier, truths of the Bible and being able to teach others the truths we receive. (Receiving a truth is more than learning facts and teaching others. It is receiving them into life experience and showing them to others by life.)

Hebrews chapter four and five introduce the Melchizedek priesthood of which we are a part (Jesus Christ being the High Priest of this order). "And having been perfected, He became the author of eternal salvation to all who obey Him, called by God as High Priest according to the order of Melchizedek; and hard to explain, since you have become dull of hearing.

For though by this time you ought to be teachers, you need someone to teach you again the first principles of the oracles of God; and you have come to need milk and not solid food. For everyone who partakes only of milk is unskilled in the word of righteousness, for he is a babe. But solid food belongs to those who are of full age, that is, those who by reason of use have their senses exercised to discern both good and evil" (Heb. 5:9-14).

Babes are self-centered. They want that which satisfies their own needs. Maturity means we have come to the status where we consider the needs of others and move to meet that need. In Hebrews 4:12 we find the word of God is able to distinguish between that which is of soul and that which is of spirit. The writer then directs our attention heavenward to the Melchizedek priesthood of Christ and to the throne of grace where we obtain mercy and find grace to help in time of need (Heb. 4:12-16). Now that we have found a place of help for our need, we can turn our attention to the need of others. In fact, we are instructed about our Great High Priest and the new covenant of which we are part (which provides boldness of access to God through the blood of Christ) and are invited to enter into the very holiest of the presence of God. To what end? That we may intercede for others.

We are to "consider one another in order to stir up love and good works" (Heb. 10:24).

Another evidence of maturity is overcoming obstacles and opposition. Believers are confronted with three areas in which we must overcome: the world, the flesh, and the devil. Overcoming is the subject of later chapters.

Chapter Five

Our Kinsman Redeemer Restoration To God's Plan and Purpose

Intro: <u>The Romance of Redemption</u> is the title of a book written by Dr. M.R. DeHann, a well known Bible teacher of a previous generation. Dr. DeHaan used the romantic story of Boaz and Ruth and her mother-in-law Naomi (in the Old Testament Book of Ruth), to illustrate the message of redemption through Jesus Christ.

The story of redemption is the Romance of the Ages. Redemption must be seen in its Biblical meaning, not common usage of the word. The words translated "redemption" in the Bible mean 1) to purchase, 2) to purchase out of the market place, and 3) to loose.

The law of God, given to Israel through Moses, provided that a person, who had gotten into debt, and, as a result, was indentured to his creditor, could be redeemed if someone would pay his debt. Another provision in the law was that property could also be redeemed (bought back).

The land allotted to the individual families by Joshua, when they entered the promised land, could not be sold forever. The closest kin of the person who had lost the land could redeem it if conditions were met. The conditions for redemption were:

1) The redeemer must be a close kinsman.
2) The redeemer must be able to pay price required.
3) The redeemer must be willing to purchase the property or release the person.

The need for redemption of man and of the earth is obvious. Man is not the same as when created by God and neither is the earth. The divine appraisal of God's creation was, "and God saw everything that He had made, and indeed it was very good" (Gen. 1:31). A few chapters later, however, it is written, "Then the Lord saw that the wickedness of man was great in the earth, and that every intent of the thoughts of his heart was only evil continually. And the Lord was sorry that He had made man on the earth, and He was grieved in His heart" (Gen. 6:5).

Solomon later observed, "Truly, this only have I found: that God made man upright, but they have sought out many schemes" (Ecc. 7:29). Man is carnal, sold under sin.

The world order that the Lord committed to Adam was a place of beauty, pleasantness, peace, plenty, joy and love. It was paradise. Now it is full of conflict, envy, jealousy, violence, strife, selfishness, greed and hatred. It is a place of sorrow, suffering and death.

Even the planet suffers. Earthquakes, storms, floods, droughts, etc. are not part of the original earth. Isaiah said, "For thus says the Lord, Who created the heavens, Who is God, Who formed the earth and made it, Who has established it, Who did not create it in vain, Who formed it to be inhabited" (Is. 45:18).

God's appointed steward and developer of earth, Adam failed to be a faithful steward and lost himself and his estate.

Satan has no legal right to this planet nor was he given jurisdiction to rule over man. He usurped the position by lying deception. Since man had sinned against God, fallen into a sinful condition, and was not able nor qualified to represent God, Satan quickly began to exert his influence over the mind of man.

God had not planned Adam's failure. It was his own choice. Neither did God plan for man to succeed as originally created. He was of the earth, earthy (1 Cor. 15:4-7). He was not God's ultimate man.

When Adam sinned against God, he lost his relationship with God. Up until sin entered, he was perfectly able to function in God's plan. Whatever God told him to do he did. He was in perfect communion with God. After sin entered he could not face God openly but hid from God in shame. Neither could he function in freedom before God. It was now necessary that the unfaithful steward be put out of his stewardship.

Adam was, himself, lost from God and he had lost his estate. His relationship was destroyed by guilt and his position forfeit because of inadequacy. His descendants were infested with the same malady. "All have sinned and fall short of the glory of God" (Rm. 3:23).

Enter now God's champanion, His Anointed. Here is the second Man, the Lord from heaven come to seek and save that which was lost. He comes as the Lamb of God to take away the sin of the world and also as the Lion of the tribe of Judah to execute judgment. He is God's Ultimate Man, God's Redeemer.

He is qualified as Kinsman Redeemer. He was born of woman. Existing in the form of God, He emptied Himself (whatever that means) and came in the likeness of man. Being found in appearance as a man, He humbled Himself and became obedient to the point of death. He is a Kinsman.

He is able to redeem. He does not redeem with silver and gold, but with His own precious blood "knowing that you were not redeemed with corruptible things, like silver or gold from your aimless conduct received by tradition from your fathers, but with the precious blood of Christ, as of a lamb without blemish and without spot" (1 Pet. 1:18, 19).

This Kinsman Redeemer is also willing to pay the price. Jesus said, just before His crucifixion, "just as the Son of Man did not come to be served, but to serve, and to give His life a ransom for many" (Mt. 20:28). He also said, "Therefore My Father loves Me, because I lay down My life that I may take it again. No one takes it from me, but I lay it down of Myself. I have power to lay it down, and I have power to take it again. This command I have received from My Father" (Jn. 10:17, 18).

The Redeemer, then, in order to rectify the situation, must restore man to fellowship with God and also restore him to his former estate of stewardship of earth. The sin debt must be paid, man must be loosed from sin's dominion, and the usurper must be removed from power.

The all knowing, all wise God knew from eternity what the situation would be and what He would do. The redemptive purpose of God was foreordained before the foundation of the world (See Acts 2:22-24 and 1 Pet. 1:18-20).

The result (wages) of man's sin against God was (and is) death (Rm. 3:23), both spiritual and physical. Spiritual death is man's alienation from God. Physical death is separation of spirit and soul from the body which results in the lifeless body returning to dust.

The Redeemer, in order to restore man, must die for him spiritually as well as physically. Christ, the Redeemer, died spiritually when He hung as a sin offering on the cross. He also died physically as evidenced by the water and blood which flowed from His side.

The scriptures say, "Christ died for our sins" (1 Cor. 15:3). They also say He died for us (in our stead) (Rm. 5:5).

In His death for our sins He removed the offense. Our conscience can be relieved of guilt by believing in this truth. In His death for us (in place or vicariously instead of us) He removed us from our sinful condition as the old man. (See Chapter Six for more on this subject.)

The adversary holds the sinner in bondage in two respects: 1) Through FEAR of death (and consequently, eternal separation from God). 2) As the old man we were in bondage to sin.

Christ delivered us from the bondage of fear of death by dying as a sacrifice for our sins. By taking the sting out of death He destroyed him that had the power of death, the devil.

"Inasmuch then as the children have partaken of flesh and blood, He Himself likewise shared in the same, that through death He might destroy him who had the power of death, that is, the devil, and release those who through fear of death were all their lifetime subject to bondage" (Heb. 2:14, 15).

Even though believers go through the experience of physical death, it is not the same as before. The main fear of dying was facing the Righteous Judge as guilty sinners (sins which were committed against the Judge Himself)! The sting of death, that which gave it its power to bring fear, was the guilt of sin. Now that the Redeemer has taken sin upon Himself, dying because of it, and then conquering death by rising from the dead, he has removed death's sting – disarming the enemy, Satan. It is the Righteous Judge Himself who has justified (declared righteous) the sinner because his guilt has been borne vicariously by the Kinsman Redeemer. What can the accuser do now? He cannot accuse us to the Judge who has justified us.

It is the righteous law of God which condemns the guilty. The penalty for breaking God's law is death. If the Kinsman Redeemer has vicariously answered for the sinner and the Righteous Judge has agreed, the law of God is satisfied. The righteousness of God, in Christ, is imputed to the sinner and he is free.

> *"O Death, where is your sting?*
> *O Hades, where is your victory?"*

"The sting of death *is* sin, and the strength of sin *is* the law. But thanks *be* to God, who gives us the victory through our Lord Jesus Christ" (1 Cor. 15:55-57).

Christ, our Blessed Redeemer, has also delivered believers from the bondage of sin. For what the law could not do in that it was weak through the flesh, God *did* by sending His own Son in the likeness of sinful flesh, on account of sin: He condemned sin in the flesh, that the righteous requirement of the law might be fulfilled in us who do not walk according to the flesh but according to the Spirit" (Rm. 8:3, 4).

The phrase "in the likeness of sinful flesh, and on account of sin" means the Son identified with sinful man so completely (though not guilty of sin Himself) he could be "numbered" with them (Is. 53:12). He died on account of sin as though He were the sinner. By His death, burial and resurrection He delivered us from the old man situation.

"Knowing this, that our old man was crucified with *Him,* that the body of sin might be done away with, that we should no longer be slaves of sin. For he who has died has been freed from sin. Now if we died with Christ, we believe that we shall also live with Him" (Rm. 6:6-8 NKJV).

Now we who believe in Him can happily sing with Fanny J. Crosby

Redeemed, how I love to proclaim it!
  Redeemed by the blood of the Lamb;
Redeemed thro' his infinite mercy,
  His child and forever I am.

The fourth verse of her beautiful hymn serves as a bridge to my next section.

I know I shall see in His beauty
  The King in whose law I delight;
Who lovingly guardeth my footsteps
  And giveth me songs in the night.

Our Hero has conquered death, hell and the grave.

"For I delivered to you first of all that which I also received: that Christ died for our sins according to the Scriptures, and that He was buried, and that He rose again the third day according to the Scriptures." (1 Cor. 15:3, 4)

When Jesus arose from the dead, He led a host of captives with Him. He also brought with Him the keys. He encouraged John on the isle of Patmos, "Do not be afraid; I am the First and the Last. I am He who lives, and was dead, and behold, I am alive forevermore. Amen. And I have the keys of Hades and Death." (Rev. 1:17, 18)

But He not only arose from the dead, He also ascended to His Father's throne:

> "John, to the seven churches which are in Asia: Grace to you and peace from Him who is and who was and who is to come, and from the seven Spirits who are before His throne, and from Jesus Christ, the faithful witness, the firstborn from the dead, and the ruler over the kings of the earth. To Him who loved us and washed us from our sins in His own blood, and has made us kings and priests to His God and Father, to Him be glory and dominion forever and ever. Amen." (Rev. 1:4-6)

This glorified Kinsman Redeemer has now been given authority over the earth. Just before He ascended to heaven, He announced to His disciples, "all authority has been given to me in heaven and on earth." (Mt. 28:18)

As was said at the beginning of this chapter, there are three Greek words translated "redeem" or "redemption" in the New Testament. One of these words means "to ransom" or "to pay the price of purchase." By the shedding of His precious blood, Jesus, our kinsman redeemer, paid our sin debt.

Another of the words translated "redeem" means "to loose." By His death, burial and resurrection, Jesus loosed us from the bondage of sin and made us his purchased possession. His blood was precious enough to pay for our release. The power of His resurrection is mighty to save us from all sin.

"But God, who is rich in mercy, because of His great love with which He loved us, 5 even when we were dead in trespasses, made us alive together with Christ (by grace you have been saved)" (Eph. 2:4,5).

"For the grace of God that brings salvation has appeared to all men, 12 teaching us that, denying ungodliness and worldly lusts, we should live soberly, righteously, and godly in the present age, 13 looking for the blessed hope and glorious appearing of our great God and Savior Jesus Christ, 14 who gave Himself for us, that He might redeem us from every lawless deed and purify for Himself His own special people, zealous for good works." (Titus 2:11-14)

With His blood He purchased those who believe in Him, they are bought with a price. Now He is in the process of bringing sons to glory by the power of His resurrection life. Eventually, He will return in glory, with those who are glorified with Him, to set things in order.

"For I consider that the sufferings of this present time are not worthy to be compared with the glory which shall be revealed in us. For the earnest expectation of the creation eagerly waits for the revealing of the sons of God. For the creation was subjected to futility, not willingly, but because of Him who subjected it in hope; because the creation itself also will be delivered from the bondage of corruption into the glorious liberty of the children of God. For we know that the whole creation groans and labors with birth pangs together until now. Not only that, but we also who have the firstfruits of the Spirit, even we ourselves groan within ourselves, eagerly waiting for the adoption, the redemption of our body." (Rm. 8:18-23)

At this present time He is preparing sons to reign with Him (bringing them to glory). This is the groaning stage. This stage will culminate in His glorious return to earth with those who are glorified with Him to set things in order and repair this damaged planet.

John the apostle (one of those who "beheld his excellent glory" on the Mt. of transfiguration) was caught up to heaven and shown scenes of what will take place in this process.

"Immediately I was in the Spirit; and behold, a throne set in heaven, and One sat on the throne. And He who sat there was like a jasper and a sardius stone in appearance; and there was a rainbow around the throne, in appearance like an emerald" (Rev. 4:2, 3). "And I saw in the right hand of Him who sat on the throne a scroll written inside and on the back, sealed with seven seals. Then I saw a strong angel proclaiming with a loud voice, "Who is worthy to open the scroll and to loose its seals?" And no one in heaven or on the earth or under the earth was able to open the scroll, or to look at it. So I wept much, because no one was found worthy to open and read the scroll, or to look at it. But one of the elders said to me, "Do not weep. Behold, the Lion of the tribe of Judah, the Root of David, has prevailed to open the scroll and to loose its seven seals." And I looked, and behold, in the midst of the throne and of the four living creatures, and in the midst of the elders, stood a Lamb as though it had been slain, having seven horns and seven eyes, which are the seven Spirits of God sent out into all the earth. Then He came and took the scroll out of the right hand of Him who sat on the throne. Now when He had taken the scroll, the four living creatures and the twenty-four elders fell down before the Lamb, each having a harp, and golden bowls full of incense, which are the prayers of the saints. And they sang a new song, saying: "You are worthy to take the scroll, And to open its seals; For You were slain, And have redeemed us to God by Your blood Out of every tribe and tongue and people and nation, And have made us kings and priests to our God; And we shall reign on the earth." (Rev. 5:1-10)

In this scene, the Lamb is also a Lion. As the "Lamb as it had been slain", He had made the sacrifice to redeem mankind unto Himself. As the Lion of the tribe of Judah, the Root of David, He is qualified to rule on earth.

He is the only One worthy (qualified) to open the seals of the scroll. Others were holy, but He is the only One qualified (worthy).

The Lamb/Lion is the Man, Christ Jesus, the Kinsman Redeemer. He is God's Man to rule on earth.

There are many interpretations of the Book of Revelation. We may not all agree on which is best, but we can all agree that the Book is "the Revelation of Jesus Christ" (Rev. 1:1).

It is not, then, merely a prophesy of coming events. If we keep in mind that it is the revelation of Jesus Christ, we may see it as Him fulfilling the eternal purpose and intent of Father, Son and Holy Spirit in their eternal counsel in which the decision was made to create man in His image and likeness and "set him over the works of God's hands."

Man was to "partner" with God. It should be abundantly clear that man "formed of the dust of the ground" (no matter how fearfully and wonderfully made) could not, without being transformed, be set over the works of God's hands. The writer of the letter to the Hebrews makes it clear that what was intended was that "he left nothing that is not put under him" (Heb. 2:8).

The only One to whom this could possibly apply was the God/Man, the Kinsman Redeemer. But with Him there will be a host of sons who will rule. These are the sons who, having suffered with Him, are glorified together with Him. They have "seen Him as He is" and are "like Him" by the transforming power of the "Spirit of life in Christ Jesus".

What we have in the Book of Revelation is Jesus, our kinsman redeemer, the Lamb of God, as the Lion of Judah, the Root of David, exercising His right and demonstrating His power to take possession of His purchase. He not only redeemed man; He also redeemed the lost position as ruler over the earth which had come under the curse because of man's sin. He is delivering God's planet earth from the adversary and his followers who have set up their sinful, God hating kingdom here.

The seven sealed scroll which the Lamb takes from the hand of Him who sits on the glorious throne of heaven is the certified deed to earth. As seals are opened, the events which occur on earth are the necessary movements to remove everything from earth that is not submitted to the will of God.

When the scroll is completely unsealed, the kingdom of this world will have become the kingdom of our God and His anointed. Jesus, man's kinsman redeemer will sit upon the throne of His glory (the throne of His Father David) until all enemies are under His feet. God and man will be united forever. God has His Man and man has his God.

Chapter Six

<u>What Ever Happened To</u>
<u>That Old Man</u>

T he term "old man" occurs three times in the New Testament, all in the writing of the apostle Paul. This phrase is usually interpreted to mean an old nature of sin within us, which we are to "put to death by crucifying ourselves", etc. This is not the interpretation used in this book. The term "old man' will be used to refer to the fallen human race which resulted from Adam's original sin and all that resulted there from.

The three New Testament references which use the term "old man" are Romans 6:6; Ephesians 4:22-24 and Colossians 3:9, 10. Dr. J. Sidlow Baxter, a Greek scholar, says that in each of these references the action spoken of is in the aorist tense, which (he says) means a once for all action which took place in the past. Romans 6:6 "Our old man <u>was</u> crucified with Him"; Colossians 3:9 "... you have put off the old man"; Ephesians 4:22 ".... You (did) put off ..... the old man". We need to know how God dealt with the old man and how that affects us.

The old man originated when Adam chose to exercise his own will contrary to the will of God. This happened in the garden of Eden when Eve ate of the forbidden fruit of the tree of the knowledge of good and evil then persuaded her husband and he ate with her. Adam, however, is held responsible, first because he is the head of the human race and secondly because, whereas Eve was deceived, Adam was not. (See 1 Tim. 2:14) This was a deliberate choice on the part of Adam to defy the rule of God and act on his own initiative.

The immediate result of Adam's action was spiritual death. Man was created to have communion with God, spirit to Spirit. Now Adam's conscience (part of his spirit) was defiled by guilt – he could no longer relate to this good God. Adam's guilt resulted from the fact that God had been good to him and Adam had disobeyed Him. God is good; Adam is not good. Sin has separated man from God. This is spiritual death.

The nature of original sin is self exaltation. Up until Adam's disobedience, he had been totally dependent upon God. When God spoke to the man he obeyed without question or hesitation. With God's command came wisdom and strength to perform whatever was commanded.

But now man had turned to his own way and must depend upon his own wisdom and strength. And they that are in the flesh cannot please God (Rm. 8:8). In this fallen state of weakness man is not able to fulfill the will and purpose of God.

The separation of man from God because of guilt is called spiritual death because the spirit of man is the faculty by which he has relationship with God. Man's conscience is the part of man that makes him aware he is guilty of wrong. His conscience is of his spirit; therefore, he is alienated from God in his spirit (spiritually dead).

God had said to the man, "Of every tree of the garden you may freely eat; but of the tree of the knowledge of good and evil you shall not eat, for in the day that you eat of it you shall surely die" (marginal reading "dying thou shalt die" KJV). This would be a favorable reading in that both spiritual death and physical death are the result of Adam's disobedience. Adam was immediately alienated from God as is evidenced in him trying to hide himself from God. Although Adam's physical life continued for hundreds of years, his eventual physical death was the result of his disobedience long ago.

In Revelation 20:14 the Bible speaks of a "second death." This death is described as being cast into the lake of fire. This is eternal separation from God. Even though spiritual death occurred before physical death, spiritual death (separation from God) is not permanent until the judgment of God after "heaven and earth" flee away (See Rev 20:11). After the final judgment, all whose names are not found written in the Book of Life are identified as "the dead" because they are dead in "trespasses and in sins" (Eph. 2:11). They were never "quickened" (made alive). They could have "taken of the water of life freely" if they would have, for Jesus offers the water of life freely (Rev. 21:6), "and the Spirit and the Bride say 'Come'! and let him who hears say, 'Come'! And let him who thirst come. Whosoever desires let him take the water of life freely" (Rev. 22:17). The fact that their names are not written in the Book of Life is proof they never came to drink of His water of Life. "And anyone not found written in the Book of Life was cast into the lake of fire." Now the condition of being alienated from God is made permanent. It is the second death because physical death occurred before spiritual death was made permanent.

Jesus, the Lamb of God, died both spiritual and physical death on the part of man. He did not experience the second death – eternal separation from God. That death is experienced by those who reject His salvation, the water of life.

The Greek word translated "sin" means "to miss the mark". Man has fallen short of the glory of God. "All have sinned and come short of the glory of God" (Rm. 3:23).

The motive and design of Satan was to disable man by making him unworthy to relate to God and isolate him so he could bring man under his influence. The lure in his solicitation was to make it appear as something good. It was good for food. It was pleasant (good) to the eye. It would make one wise (a good thing). Yes, but it was not the will of God. Adam already had what he needed – relationship with God. If he needed food God would supply. If he needed pleasantries it would be found in right relationship to God. If he needed wisdom, he could ask of God.

The hook in Satan's solicitation was "you shall be as God". God intended Adam to be "like God". He was to be holy and "have dominion". He was "of God" and he acted "for God". To be "as God", according to the "wisdom of

Satan", would place man in a position of equality with God, ruling as God on earth, placing him in competition with God instead of being God's partner in submission to God.

By yielding to the temptation, following the wisdom that does not descend from above, Adam exercised his mind of flesh and has become the enemy of God. "Because the carnal (fleshly) mind is enmity against God; for it is not subject to the law of God, nor indeed can be" (Rm. 8:7, 8).

And yet there is more. Being unworthy to fellowship with God, severed from relationship with God, (dead in trespasses and sins) man has fallen prey to the influence of the devil. He walks "according to the course of this world, according to the prince of the power of the air, the spirit who now works in the sons of disobedience", and in "the lusts of (the flesh) and of the mind, and (is) by nature the (child) of wrath..." (Eph. 2:1-3).

By yielding to the temptation of the devil, Adam inadvertently brought into being a kingdom (rule) opposed to the kingdom (rule) of God. The kingdom of God is based on the wisdom that is from above, "which is first pure, then peaceable, gentle, willing to yield, full of mercy and good fruits, without partiality and without hypocrisy" (James 3:17).

The world kingdom is based on wisdom "which does not come from above but is "earthly, sensual, demonic" ... "where there is envy, self-seeking, confusion and every evil thing" (James 3:14-18).

That is the world into which the descendants of Adam are born and of which they are a part. These sons of Adam are naturally self-centered and self-motivated. The Bible word used to describe this condition is "flesh". This is the "old man". This is what Paul refers to when he uses the term. He does not mean an old sinful nature which is in our hearts (though sin [the tendency toward evil] does dwell in us), he means the Adam race which is opposed to God, part of a world system set up in opposition to the will of God.

So here we have the wretched state of the old man: man, who was created in the image and likeness of God (and for His purpose), now fallen, living for himself, riddled with guilt, enslaved to sin, under the influence of the adversary. He is unable to rescue himself, nor can he reach God who loves him and has a wonderful plan for his life because God is Spirit and the man is carnal, sold under sin.

In addition to this, there is the awesome reality that he is accountable to God. In his heart he knows he must face the righteous judgment of God where he must give account of his stewardship. He is fearful for his shortcomings as well as his transgressions against a Holy God. He senses the wrath of God which is revealed from heaven against all ungodliness and unrighteousness of men, who suppress the truth in unrighteousness (Rm. 1:18). He knows the law of God, which is written in his heart (which expresses God's will and character), and that every transgression and disobedience must receive a just recompense of reward (Heb. 2:2 KJV). This law is holy, just and good (Rm. 7:12), but it is also uncompromising and impartial. Its demands must be satisfied and the records of men's lives, kept in God's books, are accurate and complete.

The law can be satisfied in either of two ways. 1) If it is kept perfectly, it is satisfied. 2) If it is not kept the transgressor must die.

To better understand and rightly appreciate God's dealing with the old man, we must accept God's description and evaluation of him.

The first few chapters of the Book of Genesis record the rapid degeneration and moral corruption of the human race. By the time we reach the sixth chapter we read,

Then the LORD saw that the wickedness of man *was* great in the earth, and *that* every intent of the thoughts of his heart *was* only evil continually. And the LORD was sorry that He had made man on the earth, and He was grieved in His heart. So the LORD said, "I will destroy man whom I have created from the face of the earth, both man and beast, creeping thing and birds of the air, for I am sorry that I have made them." (Gen. 6:5-7)

Note the strong words, "wickedness was great," "<u>every intent of the thoughts</u> of his heart <u>was only evil continually</u>." That was God's description of the condition of man before the flood. Even though man was but flesh, (Gen. 6:3) God dealt with him 120 years by His Holy Spirit yet there was no improvement. Only Noah who "found grace in the eyes of the Lord" (Gen. 5:8) and his family, escaped the judgment of the flood. It is also noteworthy that it was Noah who found grace in God, not the other way around. Noah was a sinner just as all the rest, but he was saved by grace through faith.

God's dealing with the sin saturated old world in the days of Noah is consistent with His dealing with the corrupt old man down through history.

When Paul presents the gospel of Jesus Christ, which is the power of God unto salvation for everyone who believes (Rm. 1:16), (which is the statement of how God saves sinners), he first proves that all men need God's gift by relating the record of man's degeneration into the depths of depravity.

"For I am not ashamed of the gospel of Christ, for it is the power of God to salvation for everyone who believes, for the Jew first and also for the Greek. For in it the righteousness of God is revealed from faith to faith; as it is written, *'The just shall live by faith.'* For the wrath of God is revealed from heaven against all ungodliness and unrighteousness of men, who suppress the truth in unrighteousness, because what may be known of God is manifest in them, for God has shown *it* to them. For since the creation of the world His invisible *attributes* are clearly seen, being understood by the things that are made, *even* His eternal power and Godhead, so that they are without excuse, because, although they knew God, they did not glorify *Him* as God, nor were thankful, but became futile in their thoughts, and their foolish hearts were darkened. Professing to be wise, they became fools, and changed the glory of the incorruptible God into an image made like corruptible man—and birds and four-footed animals and creeping things. Therefore God also gave them up to uncleanness, in the lusts of their hearts, to dishonor their bodies among themselves, who exchanged the truth of God for the lie, and worshiped and served the creature rather than the Creator, who is blessed forever. Amen. For this reason God gave them up to vile passions. For even their women exchanged the natural use for what is against nature. Likewise also the men, leaving the natural use of the woman, burned in their lust for one another, men with men committing what is shameful, and receiving in themselves the penalty of their error which was due. And even as they did not like to retain God in *their* knowledge, God gave them over to a debased mind, to do those things which are not fitting; being filled with all unrighteousness, sexual immorality, wickedness, covetousness, maliciousness; full of envy, murder, strife, deceit, evil-mindedness; *they are* whisperers, backbiters, haters of God, violent, proud, boasters, inventors of evil things, disobedient to parents, undiscerning, untrustworthy, unloving, unforgiving, unmerciful; who, knowing the righteous judgment of God, that those who practice such things are deserving of death, not only do the same but also approve of those who practice them." (Rm. 1:16-32)

No matter what God does to reveal Himself to mankind in order to bring them back to Himself, most of them continue in their own self-centered ways. God's final (and greatest) revelation of Himself was in His Son, Jesus. Most men have rejected Him. "...light has come into the world, and men loved darkness rather than light, because their deeds were evil" (Jn. 3:19).

Sinners are not going to be judged (to see if they are guilty), they are condemned already.

"For God did not send His Son into the world to condemn the world, but that the world through Him might be saved. He who believes in Him is not con-demned; but he who does not believe is condemned already, because he has not believed in the name of the only begotten Son of God. And this is the con-demnation, that the light has come into the world, and men loved darkness rather than light, because their deeds were evil. For everyone practicing evil hates the light and does not come to the light, lest his deeds should be exposed." (Jn. 3:17-20)

Paul, in his letter to the Romans, makes it clear that all are in need of salvation because all are sinners. He concludes his argument, "What then? Are we (Jews) better than they (the Gentiles)? Not at all, for we have previously charged both Jews and Greeks that they are all under sin. As it is written: 'There is none righteous, no, not one" (Rm. 3:9, 10).

In chapters three and four of Romans, we find that God justifies sinners by faith without works. Another marvelous subject is introduced in chapter four, that of imputation. Imputation is an accounting term which means to put to the account of. It can mean to either credit to the account of or debit from the account. Value may be debited from the account of one and credited to the account of another.

This doctrine explains how God, the altogether righteous One, can make sinners saints, and not violate His own holiness. He puts the sinner's sins to the account of Christ, making Him responsible for them. He also puts to the account of the sinner who believes in the Lord, the righteousness of

God in Christ (2 Cor. 5:21). Christ has already paid the debt it is now up to the sinner to believe.

These transactions all took place in the spirit realm where God's books are kept. There were a number of changes which took place when the sinner entered into these transactions by faith. The righteous law of God was completely satisfied. The sins of the sinner had been imputed to Christ who took the sinner's place and paid his debt by His death on the cross. Having been reconciled to God by the death of His Son, and having received the gift of God's righteousness, the believer is now in right standing with God and is at peace with Him. The believer also has unlimited access to God's throne of grace through the blood of Christ.

Some other changes have taken place within the believer; he has received a new heart and a new spirit. He is now indwelt by the Holy Spirit of God (the Spirit of Christ), who sheds forth the love of God in his heart and is there to make the life of Christ a motivating force within him. (See Romans chapter one through five.)

There remains one other issue, "Shall we continue in sin, that grace may abound?" The hypothetical question is answered quickly and decisively as though the question itself was unthinkable "certainly not! How shall we who died to sin live any longer in it" (Rm. 6:2)?

Sin was previously the natural habitat of the old man. He lived in it, was enslaved to it, and corrupted by it. But now the tenant has died, the slave has expired; corruption has brought him to his end. It was not some sin nature in the man that died, but the old sinner man himself who died. Sin did not die, the sinner died

The cause of the death of the old man was the corruption of sin but the implementation of the death was the crucifixion of Christ. In His infinite wisdom and great mercy, God had arranged in the heavenlies (spiritual realm) for His Son to enter the human race, take the place of Adam and his descendants in death. This is an established fact in heaven which we, as believers, must "know." By His vicarious death Christ ended Adams race as pertains to God's eternal purpose. A new man is needed.

"Or do you not know that as many of us as were baptized into Christ Jesus were baptized into His death? Therefore we were buried with Him through baptism into death, that just as Christ was raised from the dead by the glory of the Father, even so we also should walk in newness of life. For if we have been united together in the likeness of His death, certainly we also shall be in the likeness of His resurrection, knowing this, that our old man was crucified with Him, that the body of sin might be done away with, that we should no longer be slaves of sin. For he who has died has been freed from sin. Now if we died with Christ, we believe that we shall also live with Him, knowing that Christ, having been raised from the dead, dies no more. Death no longer has dominion over Him. For the death that He died, He died to sin once for all; but the life that He lives, He lives to God. Likewise you also, reckon yourselves to be dead indeed to sin, but alive to God in Christ Jesus our Lord" (Rom. 6:3-11).

Since One died for all and, therefore, all died, if God is to have a people there must be a resurrection out from the dead.

"But now Christ is risen from the dead, and has become the firstfruits of those who have fallen asleep. For since by man came death, by man came the resurrection of the dead. For as in Adam all die, even so in Christ all shall be made alive. But each one in his own order: Christ the firstfruits, afterward those who are Christ's at His coming" (1 Cor. 15:20-23).

"Those who are Christ's at His coming" lets us know that not everyone will be resurrected when Jesus comes – only those who are His. They are those who were dead in trespasses and sins, but have been made alive by accepting Christ's death as theirs and believing that God has raised Him from the dead. (See Eph. 2:1-3 and Rm. 10:9-10)

These are those who have been united to Him by death, burial and resurrection. This is the new man in Christ Jesus, the last Adam – the second Man.

Chapter Seven

<u>Who Is The New Man</u>

G od had envisioned and planned from the beginning a man with whom He could fellowship and to whom He could entrust the works of His hands. He now has that man in Jesus Christ. This is God's ultimate man, perfect in obedience and exalted to glory.

Just as the first man (Adam) was the head of the human race conformed to his image, so the second man (the last Adam – our Lord Jesus Christ) is the head of a new human race who will be conformed to His image.

"And so it is written, "The first man Adam became a living being." The last Adam became a life-giving spirit. However, the spiritual is not first, but the natural, and afterward the spiritual. The first man was of the earth, made of dust; the second Man is the Lord from heaven. As was the man of dust, so also are those who are made of dust; and as is the heavenly Man, so also are those who are heavenly. And as we have borne the image of the man of dust, we shall also bear the image of the heavenly Man" (1 Cor. 15:45-49)

We all came into being through Adam. Those who believe Jesus died for them (in their place), was buried, and was raised from the dead, are created new in Him.

Eph 2:1-10

"And you [He made alive], when you were dead (slain) by (your) trespasses and sins

In which at one time you walked (habitually). You were following the course and fashion of this world (were under the sway of the tendency of this present age), following the prince of the power of the air. (You were obedient to and under the control of) the (demon) spirit that still constantly works in the sons of disobedience (the careless, the rebellious, and the unbelieving, who go against the purposes of God).

Among these we as well as you once lived and conducted ourselves in the passions of our flesh (our behavior governed by our corrupt and sensual nature), obeying the impulses of the flesh and the thoughts of the mind (our cravings dictated by our senses and our dark imaginings). We were then by nature children of (God's) wrath and heirs of (His) indignation, like the rest of mankind.

But God — so rich is He in His mercy! Because of and in order to satisfy the great and wonderful and intense love with which He loved us,

Even when we were dead (slain) by (our own) shortcomings and trespasses, He made us alive together in fellowship and in union with Christ; (He gave us the very life of Christ Himself, the same new life with which He quickened Him, for) it is by grace (His favor and mercy which you did not deserve) that you are saved (delivered from judgment and made partakers of Christ's salvation).

And He raised us up together with Him and made us sit down together (giving us joint seating with Him) in the heavenly sphere (by virtue of our being) in Christ Jesus (the Messiah, the Anointed One).

He did this that He might clearly demonstrate through the ages to come the immeasurable (limitless, surpassing) riches of His free grace (His unmerited favor) in [His] kindness and goodness of heart toward us in Christ Jesus.

For it is by free grace (God's unmerited favor) that you are saved (delivered from judgment and made partakers of Christ's salvation) through [your] faith. And this [salvation] is not of yourselves (of your own doing, it came not through your own striving), but it is the gift of God;

Not because of works (not the fulfillment of the Law's demands), lest any man should boast. (It is not the result of what anyone can possibly do, so no one can pride himself in it or take glory to himself).

For we are God's (own) handiwork (His workmanship), recreated in Christ Jesus, (born anew) that we may do those good works which God predestined (planned beforehand) for us [taking paths which He prepared ahead of time], that we should walk in them (living the good life which He prearranged and made ready for us to live)." (Eph 2:1-10) (Kenneth S. Wuest Expanded Translation; William B. Eerdman, Publisher, Grand Rapids, Mi.)

This passage in Ephesians chapter two speaks of salvation by grace through faith. This salvation is described as; being made alive from the dead with the life of Christ by which He was raised from the dead, as being raised up together and seated with Christ in the heavenlies and of being created new in Christ.

A new creation was necessary because the old man in Adam was a fallen creature. He is described in this passage as being dead (to God) in trespasses and in sins, as following in the course of the world, as being under the control of the prince of the power of the air, the spirit which is at work in those who are opposed to God.

The main problem which made a new creation necessary was that of man's heart, the control center of his thoughts and intents (life directing decisions). The heart which had originally been centered in man's spirit, (his God consciousness), was now centered in his soul, (his self consciousness).

The grave condition of man reveals the fundamental problems with natural man and also why, in the eternal counsel of God, the decision was made for the son of God to become man, take man's place in death, and in the process bring into being a new and different humanity.

Jesus coming into the world and dying for man was not an emergency stop gap solution to a minor glitch in God's program. Had Jesus come and restored man to his original condition and status, he would only fail again. If God had done away with Adam and created another like him, that man would also have failed.

God's intention and desire from the beginning of creation was to have a being with whom He could commune and with whom He could share as a covenant partner. If such a being were to exist, God must create him in His image and likeness. Part of that likeness would be a free will. If that being had a free will he might (and would) use that freedom to choose other than the will of God.

But this mortal, fallible, man was but the first stage in development of God's man. "And so it is written, the first man Adam became a living being", the last Adam became a life giving sprit. However, the spiritual is not first, but the natural, and afterward the spiritual (that is, in the development of man).

The first man was of the earth, made of dust; the second Man is the Lord from heaven. As was the man of dust, so also are those who are made of dust; and as is the heavenly man, so also are those who are heavenly. And as we have borne the image of the man of dust, we also shall bare the image of the heavenly Man. (1 Cor. 15:45-49)

Neither was God unaware of what it would cost to bring these sons to glory. Jesus is the "Lamb slain from the foundation of the world" (Rev. 13:8). His coming into the world was for the express purpose of destroying the works of the devil and loosing man from the bondage of sin by His death, burial and resurrection. When facing the hour of His death He said, "Now my soul is troubled, and what shall I say? Father, save Me from this hour? But for this purpose I came to this hour." (Jn. 12:27)

The cross of calvary was a God – planned event. The crucifixion of Jesus did not "just happen". It was planned by God the Father, Son and Holy Spirit:

"Men of Israel, hear these words: Jesus of Nazareth, a Man attested by God to you by miracles, wonders, and signs which God did through Him in your midst, as you yourselves also know — Him, being delivered by the determined purpose and foreknowledge of God, you have taken by lawless hands, have crucified, and put to death; whom God raised up, having loosed the pains of death, because it was not possible that He should be held by it" (Acts 2:22-25).

The crucifixion was the carrying out of the determined purpose of God. It was the means by which God crucified the old man and created the new. Jesus is the "Lamb slain from the foundation of the world" (Rev. 13:8). Paul said "He (God) chose us in Him (Christ) before the foundation of the world". And Peter writes, "knowing that you were not redeemed with corruptible things like silver and gold, from your aimless conduct received by tradition from your fathers but with the precious blood of Christ, as of a lamb without blemish and without spot. He indeed was foreordained before the foundation of the world, but was manifested in these last times for you" (1 Pet. 1:18-20).

Jesus' coming into the world (becoming man, and all that that involves), was all planned before time began, "but when the fullness of the time had come, God sent forth His Son, born of woman" (Gal. 4:4), "and being found in appearance as a man, He humbled Himself and became obedient to the point of death, even the death of the cross" (Phil. 2:8).

Jesus took flesh and blood (became mortal) so He could suffer death. He had obeyed His Father in every respect up to the garden of Gethsemane. Here He experienced His final and greatest test of obedience. His father offered Him a cup to drink. The contents of this cup actually staggered this holy Man. The words used to describe His reaction and response to this cup revealed just how horrible its contents were.

His reaction indicated the cup was more than the physical death of a man crucified on a cross. That is, no doubt, a horrible way to die, but other men died on crosses. Jesus knew this was coming and what it looked like. He had talked about it to His disciples, but never reacted as He did when He took the cup from His Father's hand in the garden. Here we are told He was "exceeding sorrowful", "utterly astonished" (Mk. 14:33 Strong's Concordance), "very heavy (greatly distressed)" (Mt. 26:37) and "being in an agony (anguished)" (Lk. 22:44). The experience was such that an angel was dispatched from heaven to strengthen Him. He even pleaded with His Father, "Abba, Father, all things are possible for you, take this cup from Me" – but added, "Nevertheless, not what I will, but what you will" (Mk. 14:36).

What horrible thing was in that cup? Surely it was the composite of the filth of the combination of the sin and sinful acts of all humanity. Every corrupt act and filthy thought of the human race was in that cup, and the full extent of the sight staggered and horrified Jesus when He realized He must become that! For the Scripture says clearly, "for He made Him who knew no sin to be sin for us, that we might become the righteousness of God in Him" (2 Cor.5:21). His holy person recoiled at the very thought of becoming that! And more, if He becomes that He will be alienated from the Father. (On the cross He screamed in a loud, forlorn, voice, "Eloi, Eloi, lama sabachthni"? which is interpreted, "My God, My God, why have you forsaken Me"? Think about it! This holy One who never knew a moment of His Father's disfavor is now estranged from Him because He has become our sin! And now He stands all alone, the lamb of God, laden with our sins, and for us the sinner, "For He made Him who knew no sin to be sin for us, that we might become the righteousness of God in Him" (2 Cor. 5:21). He stands, as a sheep before His shearers without one word of protest, and as God's sacrificial lamb. Isaiah the prophet paints the poetic picture for us in Isaiah 53.

"Who has believed our report? And to whom has the arm of the LORD been revealed? For He shall grow up before Him as a tender plant, And as a root out of dry ground. He has no form or comeliness; And when we see Him, There is no beauty that we should desire Him. He is despised and rejected by men, A Man of sorrows and acquainted with grief. And we hid, as it were, our faces from Him; He was despised, and we did not esteem Him.

Surely He has borne our griefs and carried our sorrows; Yet we esteemed Him stricken, Smitten by God, and afflicted. But He was wounded for our transgressions, He was bruised for our iniquities; The chastisement for our peace was upon Him, And by His stripes we are healed. All we like sheep have gone astray; We have turned, every one, to his own way; And the LORD has laid on Him the iniquity of us all.

He was oppressed and He was afflicted, Yet He opened not His mouth; He was led as a lamb to the slaughter, And as a sheep before its shearers is silent, So He opened not His mouth. He was taken from prison and from judgment, And who will declare His generation? For He was cut off from the land of the living; For the transgressions of My people He was stricken. And they made His grave with the wicked — But with the rich at His death, Because He had done no violence, Nor was any deceit in His mouth.

Yet it pleased the LORD to bruise Him; He has put Him to grief. When You make His soul an offering for sin, He shall see His seed, He shall prolong His days, And the pleasure of the LORD shall prosper in His hand. He shall see the labor of His soul, and be satisfied. By His knowledge My righteous Servant shall justify many, For He shall bear their iniquities. Therefore I will divide Him a portion with the great, And He shall divide the spoil with the strong, Because He poured out His soul unto death, And He was numbered with the transgressors, And He bore the sin of many, And made intercession for the transgressors" (Isa 53:12).

In this prophesy, Isaiah speaks of the substitutionary, sacrificial Lamb of God. He was numbered with the transgressors, (counted as one of them), He was bruised for our iniquities, His soul was made an offering for sin, He made intercession for the transgressors, He poured out his soul unto death. But we also read of his life being extended (the resurrection), That the Lords work would prosper in His hand, and of Him seeing His seed.

He voluntarily gave His back to the smiters. Jesus said, "therefore My Father loves Me, because I lay down My life that I may take it again. No one takes it from Me, but I lay it down of Myself. I have power to lay it down, and I have power to take it again. This command have I received from My Father" (Jn. 10:17,18)

In laying His life down, He ended the old man; in taking it again He began a new man. Those who believe in His death, burial and resurrection are born again into Him by His Holy Spirit.

"Therefore, if anyone is in Christ, he is a new creation; old things have passed away; behold, all things have become new. Now all things are of God, who has reconciled us to Himself through Jesus Christ" (2 Cor. 5:17,18).

Who is this new man? What is He like? What kind of life does He live? He is born of God. "But as many as received Him, to them He gave the right to become children of God, to those who believe in His name: who were born, not of blood, nor of the will of the flesh, nor of the will of man, but of God" (Jn. 1:12,13). This new man is "created according to God, in true righteousness and holiness" (Eph. 4:24). He died, and was raised with Christ; His life is now hidden with Christ in God (Col. 3:1-4).

It is the same man (person), but he is different. Just as Jesus was different after His resurrection, so is the new man. Those who had been so intimate with Jesus in the natural found it necessary to become reacquainted with Him in the Spirit. He took forty days to be with them in His new life to help them adjust. He appeared again and again to them in bodily form to convince them of His reality. On one occasion He urged them to, "behold my hands and My feet, that it is I Myself. Handle Me and see, for a spirit does not have flesh and bones as you see I have" (Lk. 24:39).

So different was He that two of His disciples walked miles with Him, walking and talking with Him, and did not recognize Him until He expounded to them the scripture concerning Himself and as He broke bread with them (see Luke 24:13-31). Just so, the new man in Christ has a quality about Him that is different but can only be discerned in the spirit. This spirit of resurrection power operating in the new man is only an earnest of what is to be experienced in the full resurrection when Jesus returns.

The new man in Christ is the same person as before, but he is changed. Where as before he was enslaved to sin, self centered and self sufficient, dwelling in a body of sin, belonging to a world which is opposed to God; he is now set free from the bondage of sin, the body of sin has been destroyed, he is God centered, submissive, called out from the world, made the righteousness of God in Christ and seated with Him in the heavenlies.

This biblical description of the condition of the new man in Christ must be accepted by faith. These facts are absolutely true in the judicial reckoning of God. They can only be seen by faith. "For we walk by faith, not by sight" (2 Cor. 5:7). We experience these realities as we, "look not at the things which are seen; for the things which are seen are temporal; but the things which are not seen are eternal" (2 Cor. 4:18 KJV).

God uses means to bring us to the end of self dependence and self sufficiency to the place of dependence upon His resources and the abundance of the Christ life within.

"But we have this treasure in earthen vessels, that the excellence of the power may be of God and not of us. We are hard-pressed on every side, yet not crushed; we are perplexed, but not in despair; persecuted, but not forsaken; struck down, but not destroyed — always carrying about in the body the dying of the Lord Jesus, that the life of Jesus also may be manifested in our body. For we who live are always delivered to death for Jesus' sake, that the life of Jesus also may be manifested in our mortal flesh. So then death is working in us, but life in you. And since we have the same spirit of faith, according to what is written, "I believed and therefore I spoke," we also believe and therefore speak, knowing that He who raised up the Lord Jesus will also raise us up with Jesus, and will present us with you. For all things are for your sakes, that grace, having spread through the many, may cause thanksgiving to abound to the glory of God. Therefore we do not lose heart. Even though our outward man is perishing, yet the inward man is being renewed day by day. For our light affliction, which is but for a moment, is working for us a far more exceeding and eternal weight of glory, while we do not look at the things which are seen, but at the things which are not seen. For the things which are seen are temporary, but the things which are not seen are eternal" (2 Cor. 4:7-18). NKJV

The believer is left in the world in natural bodies for a reason. Just as Jesus remained here for forty days after His resurrection to persuade the unbelieving of the realities of the things which have taken place in God's scheme of things, so the justified, spiritually alive, believers (who are now citizens of the kingdom of God) are left here to be His witnesses. After the forty days with His disciples Jesus said to them, "thus it is written, and thus it was necessary for the Christ to suffer and to rise from the dead the third day, and that repentance and remission of sins should be preached in His name to all nations, beginning at Jerusalem. And you are witnesses of these things" (Lk 24:46-48).

These witnesses are not witnesses to themselves (what they are and do), but to Jesus Christ (what He is and does).

As the apostle Paul said, "for we do not preach ourselves, but Christ Jesus the Lord, and ourselves your bondservants for Jesus sake" (2 Cor. 4:5).

These sons are a work in progress, they are not yet perfect except in the predestination concept of God. They are saved by God's grace, "not by works of righteousness which we have done, but according to His mercy He saved us, through the washing of regeneration and renewing of the Holy Spirit" (Titus 3:5).

The possibility of acts of sin still exist. Sin is still in the believer, but there is a vast difference. It was natural for the old man to sin, it is unnatural for the believer to sin. Believers are to overcome sin in their members. The subject of overcoming sin will be covered more thoroughly in chapter eleven.

It shall be obvious from the truths we have seen about this man in Christ, that he is truly a new man: 1) He has a new relationship. In relation to the Father, he is a child of God, born of God. In relation to the Son, he is a brother beloved and fellow heir, one whom Christ is not ashamed to call brother. In relation to the Holy Spirit he is the temple for His indwelling. In relation to other believers, he is a brother, one with them. 2) He has a new life. Christ is now his life; he lives, but it is really Christ living in him. This life is eternal and it is holy. 3) He is under a new covenant. This is a blood covenant between God the Father and Jesus Christ. The believer, being in Christ is under that covenant. 4) He has a new heart. One of the provisions of the new covenant was a new heart, a new control center. 5) He has a new spirit, which is another provision of the new covenant. This spirit is the Spirit of Christ. He is able to commune with the creator.

The new covenant is a covenant of grace in which God says, "For I will be merciful to their unrighteousness, and their sins and their lawless deeds I will remember no more" (Heb. 8:12). The question arises, "what shall we say then? Shall we continue in sin that grace may abound?" (Rm. 6:1). The answer to this hypothetical question is quick and precise;

"Certainly not! How shall we who died to sin live any longer in it? Or do you not know that as many of us as were baptized into Christ Jesus were baptized into His death? Therefore we were buried with Him through baptism into death, that just as Christ was raised from the dead by the glory of the Father, even so we also should walk in newness of life. For if we have been united together in the likeness of His death, certainly we also shall be in the likeness of His resurrection, knowing this, that our old man was crucified with Him, that the body of sin might be done away with, that we should no longer be slaves of sin. For he who has died has been freed from sin. Now if we died with Christ, we believe that we shall also live with Him" (Rom 6:2-8). NKJV

Truly this is a new man. (More on the sixth, seventh and eighth chapters of Romans, in the chapter on overcoming the flesh). 6) The new man has a new citizenship. He is a citizen of heaven, of the kingdom of God (Phil. 3:20, 21). 7) He has a new destiny. He is to be with Christ over the works of God's hands. 8) He has a new glory. He is to share in the glory of Christ in His kingdom and glory.

The first natural man was "fearfully and wonderfully made" (Ps. 139:14). Scientists are still discovering wonderful things about the functioning of the physical body. The complex mind of man has soared to unimaginable heights of scientific discoveries. The resilience and tenacity of human endurance and resources are beyond our ability to comprehend. And yet, that is only the first stage in God's creation of man. When we begin to imagine what God has for His people the mind simply comes to an impasse. If the body formed of earthly elements is as we are beginning to discover how could we begin to imagine what the spiritual, immortal, incorruptible body of our heavenly house will be like.

"For we know that if our earthly house, this tent, is destroyed, We have a building from God, a house not made with hands, eternal in the heavens. For in this we groan, earnestly desiring to be clothed with our habitation which is from heaven, if indeed, having been clothed, we shall not be found naked. For we who are in this tent groan, being burdened, not because we want to be unclothed, but further clothed, that mortality may be swallowed up by life. Now He who has prepared us for this very thing is God, who also has given us the Spirit as a guarantee. So we are always confident, knowing that while we are at home in the body we are absent from the Lord. For we walk by faith, not by sight. We are confident, yes, well pleased rather to be absent from the body and to be present with the Lord" (2 Cor. 5:1-8). NKJV

Paul wrote, "But we speak the wisdom of God in a mystery, the hidden wisdom which God ordained before the ages for our glory, which none of the rulers of this age knew; for had they known, they would not have crucified the Lord of glory. But as it is written: "Eye has not seen, nor ear heard, Nor have entered into the heart of man the things which God has prepared for those who love Him." But God has revealed them to us through His Spirit. For the Spirit searches all things, yes, the deep things of God" (1 Cor. 2:7-10). NKJV

We can only anticipate the future with awe, "For our citizenship is in heaven, from which we also eagerly wait for the Savior, the Lord Jesus Christ, who will transform our lowly body that it may be conformed to His glorious body, according to the working by which He is able even to subdue all things to Himself" (Phil. 3:20-21). NKJV

Chapter Eight

The Church Which Is His Body

The modern concept of the church in western civilization is very different from that of the church in the beginning. The Greek word translated church is *ecclesia*, which is made up of the preposition *ek* (out of) and kaleō (to call). New Testament usage of the word includes references to a group called together to make governmental decisions and in Acts 7:38 of Israel as they had been called out of Egypt to go to their promised land.

The church is called out of the world unto Christ for His purpose. The church is more than a gathering of people. It is a body in which God, by His Spirit dwells. It is a spiritual house, the temple of God.

"In whom the whole building fitted together, grows into a holy temple in the Lord, in whom you also are being built together for a dwelling place of God in the Spirit" (Eph. 2:21, 22).

The church is an organism not an organization. An organization may have excitement, which is often called life, but it has no animation (organic life). An organization whether business, social club or educational institution may have great success as an institution or enterprise but cannot produce spiritual life. In the kingdom of God success is not measured by the numerical size of the congregation nor the popularity of the pastor, but by the force of its spiritual life. Spirit life can transform an individual, a community, an entire nation or the entire world. That is the kind of influence God is interested in. That is why He structured the church as an organism which He can inhabit.

Even though the church, as it exists in the world today, is made up of people who live in natural bodies of flesh, the life and power thereof is spiritual, not natural. Paul, in his ministering to the saints at Corinth said, "For though we walk in the flesh (fleshly bodies), we do not war according to the flesh. For the weapons of our warfare are not carnal but mighty in God for the pulling down of strongholds, casting down arguments and every high thing that exalts itself against the knowledge of God, bringing every thought into captivity to the obedience of Christ" (2 Cor. 10:3-6).

Paul also describes his approach when preaching to the lost.

"And I, brethren, when I came to you, did not come with excellence of speech or of wisdom declaring to you the testimony of God. For I determined not to know anything among you except Jesus Christ and Him crucified. I was with you in weakness, in fear, and in much trembling. And my speech and my preaching were not with persuasive words of human wisdom, but in demonstration of the Spirit and of power, that your faith should not be in the wisdom of men but in the power of God" (1 Cor. 2:1-5).

Jesus Christ, the Head of the church, is a living stone and so are those who are baptized into His body; "For by one Spirit we were all baptized into one body – whether Jews or Gentiles, whether slaves or free – and have all been made to drink into one Spirit" (1 Cor. 12:13).

"Coming to Him as to a living stone, rejected indeed by men, but chosen by God and precious, you also, as living stones, are being built up a spiritual house, a holy priesthood, to offer up spiritual sacrifices acceptable to God through Jesus Christ" (1 Pet. 2:4-5).

Those who are born of God, baptized into the body of Christ, are more than mere containers of the Christ life Spirit; they are actually joined to Him as His members. "... he who is joined to the Lord is one spirit with Him" (1 Cor. 6:17).

What does the westernized church look like today? Is there any difference in what is called the church today and a well organized, efficiently operated, successful business?

Both rely on the best location, a good promotional scheme, advertising as to location and services offered. Both need good facilities designed to house the operation and a sufficient cash flow to support the operation.

The successful business and the successful church rely on well trained talented, effervescent experienced leadership. The officers of both have been trained in some kind of educational institution or else have gotten some training experience to prepare them as leaders.

Both are "user friendly" in that they design their product to meet perceived needs in their clientele. Some even offer "specials" to entice "customers". Some of the "churches" have promoted their services as, "we have the best preaching in town" or "we have the most exciting choir/youth/children's programs". "We are the friendliest church in town".

These comparisons are sometimes dismissed with, "well, this is God's business, and that's the greatest business there is," in total disregard for biblical precedent.

How different this from the church in its beginning. If there is any formal organization it is not apparent in the Book of Acts. Yet the church was not disorganized, it was structured around the life that was in it. The Holy Spirit Himself ordered it according to His need. The common ordinary men who were the leaders were led by the Holy Spirit not trained in some formal training school or educational institution.

It is true that these eleven disciples had been in the School of Christ for about three years, but of what did this education consist? They were instructed in the higher values of the spiritual life and the exceeding high moral and ethical standards of the kingdom of heaven. Their practical training consisted of laying hands on the sick for healing, casting out demons and preaching the good news of the kingdom of God.

Jesus did announce to them He would build His church but did not tell them how to organize it or set up a church staff.

This is not to say saints should not be educated in the things of God. Every saint will be held personally responsible to learn and help others to learn all they can of the word of God. The point being made is that formal education and intense training will never replace the work of the Holy Spirit.

A notable exception of leaders having formal education is the apostle Paul. This apostle had been educated in a notable school. But after Paul met Jesus, he went into the desert for three years to be taught by the Lord Himself. The apostle refers to this experience in his letter to the Galatians.

> "But when it pleased God, who separated me from my mother's womb and called me through His grace, to reveal His Son in me, that I might preach Him among the Gentiles, I did not immediately confer with flesh and blood, nor did I go up to Jerusalem to those who were apostles before me; but I went to Arabia, and returned again to Damascus. Then after three years I went up to Jerusalem to see Peter, and remained with him fifteen days" (Gal. 1:15-18). Therefore, Paul could rightfully say, "But I make known to you, brethren, that the gospel which was preached by me was not according to man. For I neither received it

from man, nor was I taught it, but it came through the revelation of Jesus Christ" (Gal. 1:11, 12).

This does not mean, nor does the apostle infer, we should not be taught by others who have learned from the Lord. The caution is not to look to talented teachers, no matter how popular, as our authority in understanding the scriptures. They help us, but they are not the final authority. The Holy Spirit is the one who enlightens every believer.

Perhaps a quick scan of the beginning of the church and the rapid progress made in those first few months and years will help us see just how well the setup worked.

Forty days after His resurrection and just before His ascension to the Father, Jesus having gathered a number of His followers (the eleven apostles among them), commissioned them to preach the gospel to the whole world (Mk. 16:15). But He commanded them not to leave Jerusalem until they were "endued with power from on high" (Acts 1:4). This was the promise of the Father to send the Holy Spirit in a new way to indwell them. They had experienced the Holy Spirit working with them as they laid hands on the sick and had cast out demons in Jesus name. Jesus had told them of this "promise of the Father," that the Holy Spirit who had been with them would now indwell them (Jn. 14:17).

There were about one hundred twenty of them who waited prayerfully in the upper room until, on the day of Pentecost, the Holy Spirit came upon them and filled them. This event was accompanied by a series of miraculous wonders. When this was noised abroad, a multitude of people gathered, wondering what this meant.

Peter, one of the eleven, explained that this was spoken of by an old testament prophet by the name of Joel. Peter further announced to these people that the Man who had been crucified at their insistence had been resurrected by God, that He was the promised descendant, of David, and that God had exalted Him and made Him both Lord and Christ (Acts 2:1 – 36).

Upon hearing this, the people were convicted by the Holy Spirit, repented of their sins, were baptized and about three thousand of them added to the church by the Lord.

These joyful believers continued meeting daily to share with one another and continue to learn from the apostle's teaching. They were so filled with the grace of God that many who owned property sold it and gave to others who had need.

Miracles continued to happen as the apostles continued to witness Jesus' resurrection. This was met with great opposition of the Jewish leaders who threatened the apostles, commanding them not to preach in the name of Jesus, and had some of them arrested. Instead of obeying the leaders, the apostles told the congregation about the threats. They all prayed for greater boldness by increased miracles. The very place where they were assembled was shaken and they were all filled with the Holy Spirit and continued to speak the word of God with boldness (See Acts Chapters 3 & 4).

Those days were described by the following quote: "Now the multitude of those who believed were of one heart and one soul; neither did anyone say that any of the things he possessed was his own, but they had all things in common. And with great power the apostles gave witness to the resurrection of the Lord Jesus. And great grace was upon them all" (Acts 4:32, 33).

There arose a need for discipline of those within their number. Anannias and his wife Sapphira, for personal glory, misrepresented what they had done in claiming they had given all the money received from sale of their property. Peter confronted them that they had lied to the Holy Spirit, and they died on the spot for their action. To the modern church this may seem detrimental to church growth, but to the contrary we read,

> "So great fear came upon all the church and upon all who heard these things. And through the hands of the apostles many signs and wonders were done among the people. And they were all with one accord in Solomon's Porch. Yet none of the rest dared join them, but the people esteemed them highly. And believers were increasingly added to the Lord, multitudes of both men and women, so that they brought the sick out into the streets and laid them on beds and couches, that at least the shadow of Peter passing by might fall on some of them. Also a multitude gathered from the surrounding cities to Jerusalem, bringing sick people and those who were tormented by unclean spirits, and they were all healed" (Acts 5:11-16).

Things were going great. In Jerusalem the church had grown so large the apostles were not able to distribute all the money that has been laid at their feet. Some of the widows were being overlooked. Seven men were selected and appointed over this matter that the apostles may give their undivided attention to prayer and ministering the word.

"Then the word of God spread, and the number of the disciples multiplied greatly in Jerusalem, and a great many of the priests were obedient to the faith" (Acts 6:7).

Steven, one of the seven chosen to work with the apostles, "a man full of faith and power, did great wonders and signs among the people" (Acts 6:8). Some of the unbelieving Jewish leaders arranged to have Steven stoned to death. Saul of Tarsus, one of the instigators, consented to his death. A great persecution arose against the church at this time and many were killed.

Apart from the persecution and murdering of some of the disciples, everything was going great. The Jewish high priest made the charge that they had filled Jerusalem with their doctrine (Acts 5:28) and we also read,

"And through the hands of the apostles many signs and wonders were done among the people. And they were all with one accord in Solomon's Porch. Yet none of the rest dared join them, but the people esteemed them highly. And believers were increasingly added to the Lord, multitudes of both men and

women, so that they brought the sick out into the
streets and laid them on beds and couches, that at
least the shadow of Peter passing by might fall on
some of them. Also a multitude gathered from the
surrounding cities to Jerusalem, bringing sick people
and those who were tormented by unclean spirits,
and they were all healed" Acts 5:12-16).

But there is something wrong with this picture. They
have "filled Jerusalem" with their doctrine, great miracles
were being done at the hands of the apostles, the church in
Jerusalem had grown to many thousands, but they had not
done what Jesus commanded them to do – preach the gospel
in all Judea, in Samaria, and to the ends of the earth (Acts
1:8). Furthermore, the commission was given to more than
the eleven apostles. In Luke 24:33 we read, "So they rose
up that very hour and returned to Jerusalem, and found the
eleven and those who were with them gathered together."
The narration continues without interruption to these words
of Jesus, "Thus it is written, and thus it was necessary for the
Christ to suffer and to rise from the dead the third day, and
that repentance and remission of sins should be preached in
His name to all nations, beginning at Jerusalem. And you are

witnesses of these things." We are not told just how many were gathered at that time, but we do know that Paul wrote to the Corinthians that "He was seen by over five hundred brethren at once" (1 Cor. 15:6). We also know there were about one hundred twenty gathered in the upper room on the day of Pentecost who must have heard Him tell them to remain in Jerusalem until they were endued with power from on high. That endument of power would have enabled every one of them to be involved in healing the sick, casting out demons, etc. But we read they were bringing people to Peter to be healed.

> "And believers were increasingly added to the Lord, multitudes of both men and women, so that they brought the sick out into the streets and laid them on beds and couches, that at least the shadow of Peter passing by might fall on some of them. Also a multitude gathered from the surrounding cities to Jerusalem, bringing sick people and those who were tormented by unclean spirits, and they were all healed" (Acts 5:14-16).

They were making two mistakes. 1) They were bringing people in from the surrounding cities of Judea instead of planting churches in those cities. 2) They were bringing the sick and demonized to the apostles for them to do the work instead of doing it themselves. Evidence that they could have done the same works is that Stephen and Philip (later) did the same types of things the apostles had been doing (See Acts 6:8 and 8:6, 7).

When Stephen was tragically martyred and the great persecution broke out against the church, believers were scattered throughout the regions of Judea and Samaria, EXCEPT THE APOSTLES.

Our all wise God who causes "all things to work together for good to those who love Him, to those who are called according to His purpose" (Rm. 8:28), caused even these tragic events to get His will done. These who were scattered "went preaching the word" (Acts 11:19). Philip went to Samaria and a great work was begun there. Word of these things soon reached the apostles back in Jerusalem and they sent Peter and John to investigate (See Acts 8:14, 15).

Those who were scattered beyond Samaria to the regions of Phoenicia, Cyprus, and Antioch, preached the word to the Jews in those areas. Others who were from Cyprus and

Cyrene, who had been in Jerusalem on the day of Pentecost (see Acts 2:10), when they came to Antioch, spoke to the Hellenists, preaching the Lord Jesus. The hand of the Lord was with them and a great number believed and turned to the Lord (Acts 11:20, 21).

News of these things came to the ears of the church in Jerusalem and they sent Barnabas to Antioch. This was very significant because Barnabas was the individual who had believed the testimony of Saul of Tarsus when he came to Jerusalem to join the disciples but could not because they were afraid of him. Barnabas heard his testimony and introduced him to the apostles (Acts 9:26, 27).

In his testimony, Saul related how the Lord had told him he would be sent to the Gentiles as His witness to them (Acts 26:17, 18). Barnabas, seeing the Hellenists turn to the Lord, and, even though the Lord had used Peter to open the door to Gentiles (Acts 10), Barnabas remembered that Saul had been especially commissioned to witness to the Gentiles, sent to Tarsus to bring Saul to Antioch. From this church at Antioch, Saul (who became Paul) and Barnabas were sent forth to the Gentiles.

This quick review of the beginnings should help us to see what Jesus intended the church to be. Wherever these people went they preached Jesus and churches sprang up. These churches did not begin with a pastor setting up an organization.

As Paul and Barnabas went preaching the gospel from city to city (sometimes being forced to flee) the believers in each city formed a church. Some time later when these Apostles returned to Antioch, traveling through the same cities, they found the church alive and well. They encouraged them to continue in the faith and ordained elders in every city (Acts 14:21-23). Later still, Paul suggested to Barnabas, "Let us now go back and visit our brethren in every city where we have preached the word of the Lord, and see how they are doing" (Acts 15:36). Although this trip never happened, when Paul and Silas went to these churches, they found them doing well (in spite of persecution and opposition).

This historical review has been presented in an effort to show that these churches thrived without human organization. They continued and grew as a living organism led and supported by the life of the Spirit of Christ which indwelt them. There was leadership, but leadership developed by the Holy Spirit. The New Testament compares the church to the human body. The body develops around its life. Function determines the form. As the life develops, the body takes the needed form for the life to function.

This type of church has difficulty taking root in western countries. There is very little glory for the individual leader. Leadership is more incidental than something sought after. The Lord alone is exalted. The real question is not "What seems best to us" but, "what works best to accomplish God's will."

It is working in China. The joy filled church there continues to explode in growth in spite of the fact they are forced to operate underground because of China's oppressive civil government. Christians there are deprived and persecuted, many have been martyred. There is little formal organization, no well known leaders (when leaders are discovered they are imprisoned). And yet the church functions and spiritual lives are developed.

Another question to be considered concerns the <u>message</u> of the church. Has the original message delivered to the church been compromised? Most of the messages of the western church have more to do with how to be successful in this life. How to be happy! How to have a happy marriage, etc!

Surely, these are important matters and they are provided for in the Bible. But, scripturally speaking these are side issues. The Biblical approach is to help saints to know what they have in Christ and who He is in them.

Anyone living the Christ life which resides in the believer (the grace life) and who knows what they are in Christ (more than conquerors) will be successful in life (by Bible standards of success) and will have a happy marriage because Christ is first in the life of both husband and wife and each is concerned about the welfare of the other (rather than being self centered).

The message for the church is the gospel of the grace of God. It is the grace of God that "teaches (and thus enables) us that, denying ungodliness and worldly lusts, we should live soberly, righteously, and godly in this present age, looking for the blessed hope and glorious appearing of our great God and Saviour Jesus Christ" (Titus 2:12, 13).

Central to the preaching of the gospel of the grace of God under the anointing of the Holy Spirit is the preaching of the cross of Christ – what was accomplished there on behalf of and in the life of the believer. It is the work of the Holy Spirit to, "guide (us) into all truth," and to "glorify (Christ) (as He takes of what is (Christ's) and declares it to (us). (See Jn. 16:13-14.) As believers "walk in the Spirit (they) shall not fulfill the lusts of the flesh" (Gal. 5:16). Making practical application of these truths is the work of the Holy Spirit, not the preacher. When the preacher does it, the emphasis is on the individual applying principles and techniques to be successful, when the Holy Spirit makes application to practical living it is "Not I, but Christ who lives in me" (Gal. 2:20).

This is the message Paul preached to believers. This is the message he so strongly defended in his letter to those in Galatia.

We are saved by grace, not by works. "For by grace you have been saved through faith, and that not of yourselves; it is the gift of God, not of works, lest anyone should boast" (Eph. 2:8-9). We have no confidence in our own ability, "For we are the circumcision who worship God in the spirit, rejoice in Christ Jesus, and have no confidence in the flesh" (Phil. 3:3).

We are not "the old man which grows corrupt according to the deceitful lusts" (Eph. 4:22). We are "the new man which was created according to God, in true righteousness and holiness" (Eph. 4:24).

The primary message committed to the church to take to the world is the gospel of the kingdom. These two (the gospel of the grace of God and the gospel of the kingdom of God) are not mutually exclusive but are inclusive one of the other.

Just as the preaching of the cross is central to the gospel of grace, so it is also central to the gospel of the kingdom. The cross is the way of entrance into the kingdom and is also the basic principle upon which the kingdom operates.

The difference is the emphasis in application. The gospel of grace is the emphasis to believers; the gospel of the kingdom is the emphasis to the unbeliever. The darkened mind of the prideful unbeliever may not be impressed by the message of God's grace, but it can be shocked into attention at the message that God is bringing in His King to set up His righteous kingdom and the sinner is part of a rule that opposes God's King.

This was the message that brought conviction of the Holy Spirit to the hearts of Jewish people on the day of Pentecost. The essence of Peter's message was that God had sent His Messiah, His Saviour/King, and they had crucified Him. But that did not change the message of the kingdom. God raised Him from the dead and exalted Him to His right hand. Peter concludes his remarks with these words, "Therefore let all the house of Israel know assuredly that God has made this Jesus, whom you crucified, both Lord and Christ" (Acts 2:36). The results? "Now when they heard this, they were cut to the heart, and said to Peter and the rest of the apostles; Men and brethren, what shall we do?" (Acts 2:37)

Examples of preaching which emphasize the gospel of the kingdom when addressing unbelievers go right through the Gospels and the Book of Acts. John the Baptist (Mt. 3:12); Jesus (Mt. 4:17); the twelve whom Jesus sent out (Mt. 10:6, 7); Paul at Rome (Acts 28:23, 30, 31); and end time preachers (Mt. 24:14).

Paul, when addressing the elders of the church of Ephesus used both phrases when describing his preaching.

"But none of these things move me; nor do I count my life dear to myself, so that I may finish my race with joy, and the ministry which I received from the Lord Jesus, to testify to the gospel of the grace of God. And indeed, now I know that you all, among whom I have gone preaching the kingdom of God will see my face no more" (Acts 20:24, 25).

The work of the church is also different when dealing with those without than those within.

Toward those without (of the world), the church is to be Christ's witnesses. Jesus said to those gathered with Him when He ascended, "But you shall receive power when the Holy Spirit has come upon you, and you shall be witnesses to Me in Jerusalem, and in all Judah and Samaria, and to the end of the earth" (Acts 1:8).

Believers witness Christ to the world. To be a witness to something or someone requires first hand knowledge of the event or the person. The Greek word translated *"witness"* has been transliterated into English *"Martyr."* We call someone a martyr when they are committed to something to the extent their life is given for it (because they refuse to deny the thing). Martyrs for Jesus are usually those (like Stephen) who give their physical lives because of their stand for or commitment to Christ. Jesus used the word in such a way as to include those who are committed to Him to the extent they have given up their lives for Him. By their stand for or commitment to Christ they have forfeited their lives for Him. They will live or die for Him. They do not consider their lives to be their own.

Those who are witnesses to Him always point to Him. They point to Him as John the Baptist did, saying, "I am not the One, He is." For that stand, refusing to deny Him, they may be killed. Paul said in Rm. 8:26, "As it is written: For your sake we are killed all the day long; we are accounted as sheep for the slaughter."

Faithful witnesses, by giving up their lives to witness to Christ by word and deed, point others to Christ that they might know Him.

Another aspect of the work of the church to those without is as His Ambassadors.

"Now all things are of God, who has reconciled us to Himself through Jesus Christ, and has given us the ministry of reconciliation, that is, that God was in Christ reconciling the world to Himself, not imputing their trespasses to them, and has committed to us the word of reconciliation. Now then, we are ambassadors for Christ, as though God were pleading through us: we implore you on Christ's behalf, be reconciled to God" (2 Cor. 5:18-20).

Ambassadorship is not an insignificant position. An ambassador is one who represents his government or his king. In this case we are privileged to represent our King (Jesus) to the world. The message we bring to the people of this world is that reconciliation has been made, that is, the one offended (God) who had every right to retaliate against His rebellious people, has, by the sacrifice of His Son, taken care of the offense, and now all who will may return to Him and be gladly received. The ministry of the church (as His ambassadors) is to go to mankind in His name, announce the good news of reconciliation and plead with them to be reconciled to God. It is possible they will not receive the ambassador's message and may even mistreat them, but even that is a great privilege considering the message they bring.

Seeing the minds of the lost are blinded and their hearts so hardened (callous) and distrustful, the church has the additional work of intercession. Intercessors are those who stand in the place of and plead on behalf of another. The intercessor is asked to take the place of discomfort for the other while the hard heart, stiff neck and blinded eyes of the sinner are being dealt with. The intercessor is allowed to take upon himself a measure of the sinner's burden. Hopefully, the extension of opportunity to repent and the continued conviction of the Holy Spirit will bring the sinner to repentance.

There is also a work of the church to those within, i.e. those who are members of the same body. "So we, being many, are one body in Christ, and individually members one of another" (Rm. 12:5).

Many New Testament scriptures speak of believers responsibility to one another. Believers are to encourage each other, edify one another, exhort the brethren, warn the way-ward, etc. We are told in First Corinthians 12:24-26, "But God composed the body, having given greater honor to the part which lacks it, that there should be no schism in the body, but that the members should have the same care one for another. And if one member suffers, all the members suffer with it; or if one member is honored, all the members rejoice with it." We are to "by love serve one another" (Gal. 5:17).

The body of Christ (the church) is designed to accomplish its purpose on earth by all the members working together, each part functioning, according to its design, doing what it was designed to do. Confusion and disharmony is the fruit of members trying to perform ministries for which they were not designed.

The body of Christ, just as does the human body, has but one head. The scriptures make it abundantly clear who is the head of the church. "And He (Christ) is the head of the body, the church" (Col. 1:18). "And He (God) put all things under His (Christ's) feet, and gave Him (Christ) to be head over all things to the church, which is His body, the fullness of Him who fills all things" (Eph. 1:22, 23).

Jesus designed His body, the church, in such a way that every member should be involved, in that way every member grows into maturity. He gifted the church with men who could equip the saints for this ministry. (See Eph. 4:9-12) These men are extensions of Himself to minister to the saints "till we all come to the unity of the faith and of the knowledge of the Son of God, to a perfect man, to the measure of the stature of the fullness of Christ; that we should no longer be children, tossed to and fro and carried about with every wind of doctrine, by the trickery of men, in the cunning craftiness of deceitful plotting, but, speaking the truth in love, may grow up in all things into Him who is the head – Christ – from whom the whole body, joined and knit together by what every joint supplies, according to the effective working by which every part does its share, causes growth of the body for the edifying of itself in love" (Eph 4:13-16).

Churches with large congregations may not provide adequate opportunity for the spiritual development of individual believers. Most of the leaders of these large congregations probably desire every member be involved. In actuality however, most never do. Even when these members do become involved, it is usually in some aspect of "church work" which has little or nothing to do with spiritual development.

Some churches have developed some type of smaller group meetings in addition to their large congregation meetings. This helps if the Holy Spirit is allowed to function freely to involve members in body ministry. Body ministry allows individual members to function according to the way the Lord designed them.

When the church began at Jerusalem, it numbered into the thousands in just a few weeks. They could not have congregated in a building for "church services," there were few (if any) buildings that could house that many people. Church buildings, as such, were not constructed for almost three hundred years. They met in houses.

Even though they were at the temple every day it is not likely they met for church services. The High Priest would not have allowed that. They were sharing the good news with those Jews who came there. There was no doubt, great rejoicing and much praise, but not organized worship services. The same thing applies to meeting at the Jewish Synagogues. They gathered with the Jews to try to convince them that Jesus was the Messiah.

Believers need to be constantly reminded of the fact, "we must all appear before the judgment seat of Christ, that each one may receive the things done in the body, whether good or bad" (2 Cor. 5:10). That, "each of us shall give account of himself to God" (Rm. 14:12).

At that final exam, it is not likely that one of the questions will be, "Did you attend a good Bible believing church?" or, "What did you do to help the pastor reach his goals?" etc.

The question will probably have to do with how well we fulfilled our stewardship. It is wisdom, then, for each believer to discover what body part he is and function faithfully as that. (Romans Chapter Twelve gives a good list of categories of spiritual ministry for which believers are gifted of God. We can prove what God's "good, acceptable and perfect" will is by a presentation of our bodies (entire selves) to God (Rm. 12:1-8).

The church, as the Lord's body on earth, is to continue to do His work, suffering with Him. When He returns to take her away unto Himself, she will be glorified as His holy bride.

Chapter Nine

<u>Overcoming To Reign</u>

S ons who have been brought to glory are overcomers. Jesus said, "To him who overcomes I will grant to sit with Me on My throne, as I also overcame and sat down with My Father on His throne" (Rev. 3:21). It is overcoming that qualifies one to reign with Christ. Reigning with Him is also the reward for faithfulness. This accomplishment, then, is very important in the life of the believer.

The word means to be victorious," which infers there was conflict, resistance or opposition of some kind. It might mean a person was under the power of another but escaped. It could also mean the person accomplished a goal in spite of great opposition or resistance.

These areas in which believers are to overcome are the world, the flesh, and the devil. Overcoming is possible; else Jesus would have spoken an empty promise.

Jesus Himself overcame. In His case He was never under the world, the flesh or the devil, but He overcame them by not allowing Himself to be brought under them. By His overcoming life He qualifies to strengthen us to maintain a life of victory. Paul urges us to "stand fast therefore in the liberty by which Christ has made us free, and be not entangled again with a yoke of bondage" (Gal. 5:1).

Jesus said, "These things I have spoken unto you, that in Me you may have peace. In the world you will have tribulation; but be of good cheer, I have overcome the world" (Jn. 16:33).

He also announced what the attitude of the world would be toward His followers after He left and revealed why they hated Him so.

"If the world hates you, you know that it hated Me before it hated you. If you were of the world, the world would love its own. Yet because you are not of the world, but I chose you out of the world, therefore the world hates you. Remember the word that I said to you, 'A servant is not greater than his master.' If they persecuted Me, they will also persecute you. If they kept My word, they will keep yours also. But all these things they will do to you for My name's sake, because they do not know Him who sent Me. If I had not come and spoken to them, they would have no sin, but now they have no excuse for their sin. He who hates Me hates My Father also. If I had not done among them the works which no one else did, they would have no sin; but now they have seen and also hated both Me and My Father. But this happened that the word might be fulfilled which is written in their law, 'They hated Me without a cause" (Jn. 15:18-25).

They hated Him because He revealed their unrighteousness by His Holy life and preaching of the truth. His followers will be treated the same as He, as they follow His lifestyle.

When Jesus said to His disciples, "I will no longer talk much with you, for the ruler of this world comes, and he has nothing in Me" (Jn. 14:30). He was saying He Himself had no sin indwelling Him. There was no Satanic representative in Him. Jesus had earlier challenged His (self-righteous) enemies, "Which of you convicts Me of sin" (Jn. 8:46).

Paul speaks of "sin which dwells in me" (Rm 7:20). The reason men commit acts of sin is because sin (the inclination and desire to do that which satisfies the lower part of our nature) is in them. This evil that lives in mankind developed when Adam turned to his own selfish desires instead of what God wanted him to do. It is sometimes called "the flesh" (not the physical body but that which is of the mind and will apart from God).

All men who descended from Adam have this inherited trait. Jesus, who was born of His Father God and Mary had no "sin" dwelling in Him. He overcame "the flesh" (sin) by not yielding to His own human mind and will (as Adam had done). He "resisted unto blood" (Heb. 12:4) in the garden of Gethsemane, but He never yielded. Thus He overcame the flesh.

Jesus also overcame the devil. He resisted every offer the devil made to get Him to disobey His Father. Eventually, when He was made an "offering for sin" (Is. 53:10), and when "He who knew no sin (was made) to be sin for us" (2 Cor. 5:21), He died, and "through death He (destroyed) him who had the power of death, that is, the devil" (Heb. 2:14). The word translated "destroy" in this verse can also be translated "rendered ineffective." The devil is no longer able to do as he once did with those who are in Christ. He has been overcome.

Not only did Jesus overcome; He has made it possible for those who believe in Him to likewise overcome. It is through overcoming enemies, opposition and resistance that believers are conditioned and equipped to reign with Christ in His glorious kingdom. That is why James admonishes believers to "count it all joy when you fall into various trials" (James 1:2). Through the testing of our faith we learn to be patient (endure without giving up). Patience makes us perfect (complete, mature). (See James 1:2-4.) It is in going through these experiences that we turn to God for wisdom. True wisdom knows what the will of the Lord is. "Therefore do not be unwise, but understand what the will of the Lord is" (Eph. 5:17). God allows trials and temptations to teach us not to rely upon our own way, but to seek God's way of wisdom. "Therefore let him who thinks he stands take heed lest he fall. No temptation has overtaken you except such as is common to man; but God is faithful, who will not allow you to be tempted beyond what you are able, but with the temptation will also make the way of escape, that you may be able to bear it" (1 Cor. 10:12, 13).

Believers need to be aware of what is really happening. According to the Bible, we are involved in a great spiritual war. Furthermore the outcome of the war has already been determined. The kingdoms of this world become the kingdom of our Lord and of His Christ (Rev. 11:15). This being the case, we might wonder why the war is being fought at all. If we simply say the devil is too stupid to know he can't defeat God that would not be a complete answer. God knows the devil's limitation as well as His own power. He could annihilate the devil with one breath of His nostril.

The full answer has to do with the development of the saints. Surely He does not depend upon our help. There is not the slightest possibility He might lose if we do not do well. No, it is for us that God allows this war to go on! He wants us to be convinced we need His strength.

We are instructed in the conclusion of Paul's letter to the Ephesians:

"Finally, my brethren, be strong in the Lord and in the power of His might. Put on the whole armor of God, that you may be able to stand against the wiles of the devil. For we do not wrestle against flesh and blood, but against principalities, against powers, against the rulers of the darkness of this age, against spiritual hosts of wickedness in the heavenly places. Therefore take up the whole armor of God, that you may be able to withstand in the evil day, and having done all, to stand" (Eph. 6:10-13).

"Having done all, to stand" means to stand victorious. We also read in 2 Corinthians, "For though we walk in the flesh, we do not war according to the flesh. For the weapons of our warfare are not carnal but mighty in God for pulling down strongholds" (2 Cor. 10:3, 4).

Even though believers live on the same earth and in the same area as those who constitute the world system, they are no longer of it. They have been delivered from the power of this darkness and have been translated into the kingdom of God's beloved Son (Col. 1:13). Jesus has chosen them out of the world system, and called them unto Himself (Jn. 15:19).

The system of this world is opposed to the kingdom of God. It is not in submission to His loving rule and it attempts to exist without Him. That explains why it is full of strife and envy. The basic rule is to provide for yourself. Selfishness is the foundation of its existence.

The kingdom of God is totally opposite of the kingdoms of this world. Love, which seeks not its own and is not jealous is its basic rule. Its motive is to seek the welfare of others. Those who are translated into this kingdom must learn to live by its laws. The method of its operation is sowing and reaping.

These sons of God must learn to trust their Father as their Provider. They are to look to Him for wisdom, for vitality and for increase. In His wisdom He gives them ideas and expertise. By His Spirit He gives them vitality, integrity and favour. He makes the work of their hands to prosper.

When these sons of the kingdom have learned not to be anxious and not to turn to the ways of this world, they have overcome it (they have come out from under its control and live above it).

The flesh must also be overcome. The flesh, as it is used to mean that which lusts against the spirit and is contrary to it, (Gal. 5:17) is still in the saint but is no longer his master (Rm. 8:12). By learning to live by grace instead of attempting to keep the law but to walk in the Spirit, the believer does not fulfill the lust of the flesh (See Gal. 5:16-18). He has, in so doing, overcome the flesh.

The world system of evil, which operates today on planet earth, is Satan's mock kingdom which is set up in opposition to the righteous kingdom of God. The flesh is Satan's stronghold in individuals. When the believer gains victory over the world and over the flesh, he has eliminated Satan's power to operate in his life.

Attacks still come from Satan in the form of solicitation to entice the believer to disobey God and act to satisfy his own fleshly lusts. If he succeeds, he gains temporary victory in the believer because his conscience accuses him until he confesses his sin and receives cleansing through the shed blood of Christ.

Other trials come when Satan stirs up people to verbally and/or physically attack the saints for their righteous stand on issues and for the name of Jesus. Victory comes in these cases when the believer, rather than groveling in self-pity, rejoices at the privilege of suffering for Christ (Acts 5:41).

Jesus said, "Blessed are you when men hate you, and cast out your name as evil, for the Son of Man's sake. Rejoice in that day and leap for joy! For indeed our reward is great in heaven, for in like manner their fathers did to the prophets" (Lk. 6:22, 23). Peter also referred to this when he wrote, "Beloved, do not think it strange concerning the fiery trial which is to try you, as though some strange thing happened to you; but rejoice to the extend that you partake of Christ's sufferings, that when His glory is revealed, you may also be glad with exceeding joy.

If you are reproached for the name of Christ, blessed are you, for the Spirit of glory and of God rests upon you. On their part He is blasphemed, but on your part He is glorified" (1 Pet. 4:12-14).

The believer's warfare and way to victory is beautifully presented in Martin Luther's great hymn:

A Mighty Fortress Is Our God

A mighty fortress is our God,
A bulwark never failing;
Our helper he, a-mid the flood
Of mortal ills prevailing:

For still our ancient foe
Doth seek to work us woe;
His craft and pow'r are great,
And armed with cruel hate,
On earth is not his equal.

Did we in our own strength confide,

    Our striving would be losing;

Were not the right Man on our side,

    The Man of God's own choosing:

Dost ask who that may be?

    Christ Jesus, it is he;

Lord Sabaoth, his name,

    From age to age the same,

And he must win the battle.

And tho this world, with devils filled,

    Should threaten to undo us,

We will not fear, for God hath willed

    His truth to triumph thro' us;

The Prince of Darkness grim,

    We tremble not for him;

His rage we can endure,

    For lo, his doom is sure

One little word shall fell him.

That word above all earthly pow'rs,

No thanks to them, abideth;

The Spirit and the gifts are ours

Thro' him who with us sideth:

Let goods and kindred go,

This mortal life also;

The body they may kill:

God's truth abideth still,

His kingdom is forever.

These struggles and trials are on-the-job training. We are being brought to glory to reign with Christ. Evidence that we have overcome and are walking in victory is that we are willing to suffer for Jesus sake. We no longer defend ourselves or fight for our rights. We only resist when our King gives us orders to do so.

Paul spoke of his sacrificial lifestyle as, "...my sufferings for you and fill up in my flesh what is lacking in the afflictions of Christ, for the sake of His body, which is the church" (Col. 1:24). He also spoke of these sufferings when he wrote, "Therefore we do not lose heart. Even though our outward man is perishing, yet the inward man is being renewed day by day. For our light affliction, which is but for a moment, is working for us a far more exceeding and eternal weight of glory, while we do not look at the things that are seen, but at the things that are not seen. For the things which are seen are temporary, but the things which are not seen are eternal" (2 Cor. 4:16-18).

Reigning with Christ is not just a status symbol. It is a position of highest honor and of great responsibility. That honor and those responsibilities are for those who suffer with Christ and have overcome.

Chapter Ten

The World We Overcome

"For whatever is born of God overcomes the world. And this is the victory that has overcome the world — our faith. Who is he who overcomes the world, but he who believes that Jesus is the Son of God"? (1 John 5:4-5) NKJV

God is in the process of bringing sons to glory. He is maturing children (Gr Teknon) into sons (huios). This process involves placing His children in situations where they are confronted by opposing forces. These opposing forces are the world, the flesh and the devil. Through overcoming these forces the child is matured into manhood, the likeness of Christ.

Just as in the natural, maturity is normal and retarded growth is abnormal, so in the spiritual. God cannot release management of His creation into the hands of children. Children are not expected to consistently make wise decisions. To those who are mature, who walk in love, who are full of wisdom and who have learned how to walk in submission and obedience to Christ; to them God will entrust the care of His creation.

Believers, then, are to overcome the world. We need to know what the bible teaches about this world. There are different Greek words which are translated world in our English Bibles. The word we are primarily dealing with here is the Greek word Kosmos. That word means "an orderly arrangement" when used as a noun, and "to set in order" when used as a verb.

This word Kosmos is used in Jn. 3:16 where we read that, "God so loved the world (Kosmos) that He gave His only begotten Son, that whoever believes in Him should not perish, but have everlasting life." The same Greek word is translated world in 1 Jn 2:15,16, "do not love the world (Kosmos) or the things in the world. If anyone loves the world the love of the Father is not in Him." Obviously, these are not the same. The world that God loves is that "orderly arrangement" of His original creation, including man.

God's original creation was organized into an orderly arrangement. The stars sang together. "for thus says the Lord, who created the heavens, who is God, who formed the earth and made it, who has established it, who did not create it in vain, who formed it to be inhabited." (Is. 45:18) When He had set things in order, He created man in His own image and likeness, He prepared a beautiful garden and then placed the man in the garden instructing him to be fruitful, multiply and have dominion. This was God's world – harmonious, peaceful and in order.

Tragically, Adam turned away from God to himself, became enslaved to sin and lost his stewardship. Satan, God's adversary, took advantage of the situation and, by lies and deception, and by sowing seeds of hate, and selfishness, created the self centered, contentious, cruel, chaotic, rebellious, anti God system we see on God's earth today. This condition reigns among men today.

This system is spoken of in Eph. 2:2, "in which you once walked according to the course of this world, according to the prince of the power of the air, the spirit who now works in the sons of disobedience, among whom also we all once conducted ourselves in the lusts of our flesh, fulfilling the desires of the flesh and of the mind, and were by nature children of wrath, just as the others."

This system, which is opposed to the righteous government of God, is called the world (Kosmos – orderly arrangement) because it is ordered in such a way as to oppose God, has a certain course it follows, and has a leader. It is organized as in "organized crime." In contrast to the kingdom of God, this dark "kingdom" is full of strife, envy, and debate. It is characterized by hatred, violence and greed. The motivating force of this world system is the spirit of selfishness. Taking advantage of others, using others and dominating others is it's method of operation, using whatever means nessary to make self look good, advance self or make self feel good.

The strife, envy, lies and competition which characterizes this system is to be found in every activity organized among men of this world. It is found in business, in politics (government), social intercourse, educational institutions, religious organizations, and entertainment. Overcoming the world systems while in this life helps qualify us to reign with Christ in His coming kingdom. Jesus promised, "And he who overcomes, and keeps My works until the end, to him I will give power over the nations" (Rev. 2:26).

And again, "To him who overcomes I will grant to sit with Me on My throne, as I also overcame and sat down with My Father on His throne" (Rev 3:21). When we have overcome the world, we are no longer dependent upon its methods, under its influence or control. We are still in the world but not of the system. We were born into the system and grew up to be involved in it. Our thinking, our plans and goals were of the world. We were dependent upon it for our sustenance and our success. Jesus was not born a part of the system nor enslaved to it. He was tempted to submit Himself to it, to become part of it (a leader of it), but He resisted the temptation, remaining in submission to and obedient to His Father.

He said to His followers, "These things I have spoken to you, that in Me you may have peace. In the world you will have tribulation; but be of good cheer, I have overcome the world" (Jn 16:33). They had been of the world until He called them out of it. He said to them, "These things I command you, that you love one another. If the world hates you, you know that it hated Me before it hated you. If you were of the world, the world would love its own. Yet because you are not of the world, but I chose you out of the world, therefore the world hates you. Remember the word that I said to you, a servant is not greater than his master. If they persecuted Me, they will also persecute you. If they kept My word, they will keep yours also" (Jn 15:17-20).

As believers, we are no longer of this world because, "He has delivered us from the power of darkness and conveyed us into the kingdom of the Son of His love" (Col. 1:13). The kingdom of the Son of His love is the kingdom of heaven.

The sermon on the mount, recorded in Matthew chapters 5-7 has been called "the manifesto of the kingdom of heaven." In this manifesto are recorded motives, attitudes, nature and provisions within this kingdom. We are now citizens of this heavenly kingdom.

By His Spirit we are born into this spiritual kingdom. In this transitional period (from our new birth until the full manifestation of the kingdom on earth) we are in the process of learning how the laws of this kingdom operate within our hearts, about its economic and social affairs. Being citizens of the heavenly kingdom requires new methods and new thinking.

When we have successfully transitioned from the world system and are submitted to our King, walking by His spirit, when we are no longer under the influence and control of the world system in reference to moral and ethical standards, business practices, etc., we are overcomers.

How do we, as citizens of the heavenly kingdom, relate to earthly ruler? We recognize that all governmental authority is of God. These rulers are His representatives. We are, therefore, to submit to their authority as unto the Lord as long as they represent Him. When they depart from what is according to His word, we are to remain in a submissive attitude, but refuse to obey their orders. For instance: should these authorities command us not to speak in the name of Jesus or about Him, we must respectfully continue to obey God rather than men. We may be called upon to suffer for Him the consequences of our action or disobedience, in which case we are to take it joyfully and humbly.

If an employee were required by his supervisor to misrepresent the product or lie for the employer, they must refuse to do so bearing witness for our Lord. In these cases (which could be multiplied many times over) these heavenly citizens have overcome. Should a believer be placed in position of governing, they must make decisions and take action according to the higher standards of the heavenly kingdom. Believers should become involved in the governmental process, according to the will and leading of the Lord.

What about economics of the kingdom of heaven? Jesus said His followers should "leave all" and "seek first the kingdom of God and His righteousness, and all these things (what we eat, what we wear etc.) would be added to us" (Mt 6:19-34). Is Jesus saying believers are not to work, nor to conduct business? No, Jesus is referring to priorities and attitudes. We are to trust God and represent Him in all we do. Instead of competing with others in business, trying to take from others for ourselves, looking for self advancement above others, we are to give to others, prefer the advancement of others before ourselves. We apply ourselves diligently, doing quality work and doing a full day's work as unto the Lord. Our promotion comes from Him.

The principles of the world systems is to get everything you can; in the kingdom of which we are citizens it is to give everything you can, "give and it shall be given unto you." The Lord is our provider and our promoter. Love and respect are the governing principles of the overcomer in relating to others in society, in honor preferring one another. When we are able to live by this method, we have overcome in the business world.

What about entertainment? The better word to use here is amusement. Both words when used in this sense means "to occupy the attention." Why would believers seek for things to occupy our attention away from the Lord? In His word He tells us "you will keep him in perfect peace, whose mind is stayed on you, because he trusts in you" (Is. 26:3). Shalom, the word translated peace in this verse means "a sense of well being, happy, prosperous, healthy, complete." Why would we seek for that which takes us away from such a blessing? Obviously, Christians should abstain from anything immoral, or which promotes violence or which glorifies greed. But what about movies, music, athletics, theater etc.? We must be careful not to judge one another in these matters. Let us judge for ourselves if the activity itself or our absorption in it distracts our attention from the Lord. Our conscience must be kept undefiled.

Overcoming in this area means not being addicted to anything other than our Lord. Churches which use such activities to attract people should know that only the Spirit of Christ can draw people to Him. It is sad to see worldly attitudes and worldly principles operating in the church. In great humility of mind we must confess worldliness in what is called "the church." To a large degree church organizations (called churches) compete with each other for members, for money, for recognition. We are even told, "the church is God's business, the greatest business on earth." That would seem to be foreign to the Bible where the church is called His body, His temple, His building, His farm (to bring forth fruit), and a few other things, but where is it called a business? It isn't even referred to as an organization but an organism.

Many (so called) churches may be more like a "den of thieves" than a "house of prayer." Money seems to be the main concern in many churches. Most of the money is required to keep the organization functioning. Churches advertise for members in the same way worldly businesses promote their wares to get more customers.

What is the solution? Let the church be His body through which He works, His temple to house His spirit. Let the emphasis be on promoting His kingdom rather than our kingdom (which we call "our" church). (The only person in the Bible who ever referred to the gathering as "My" church was Jesus Himself. Let us seek His kingdom while He builds His church!)

We must overcome this worldliness in the church if we are to reign with Him on His throne. You will find it true: if you seek only His kingdom, allowing Him to be your King, doing things His way, you will be persecuted by the worldly system, especially that within what is commonly called the church. We know we have overcome this world system when we are living by faith in the Lord; When we are looking to Him for our provisions, for approval (and not to men). The overcomers measure of success is to be all he can be and do the best job he can do. We have overcome when we are at peace within and without and when love is the motivation in all we do.

The way we overcome the world is by making a complete surrender of ourselves and our future to the Lord. Let us enter at once into His rest.

"There remains therefore a rest for the people of God. For he who has entered His rest has himself also ceased from his works as God did from His. Let us therefore be diligent to enter that rest, lest anyone fall according to the same example of disobedience." (Heb 4:9-11)

Chapter Eleven

The Flesh We Overcome

Those of us who are born of God, who have been delivered from the power of darkness and have been translated into the kingdom of God's dear Son (Col. 1:13 KJV), are left here in this world on purpose. We were of the world but have been called out of it and are now sojourners and pilgrims in it.

We began this new life in Christ as newborn babes. We are meant to grow into maturity, and, in the process, be His witnesses of the Christ whose life is in us.

"As newborn babes, desire the pure milk of the word, that you may grow thereby, if indeed you have tasted that the Lord is gracious. Coming to Him as to a living stone, rejected indeed by men, but chosen by God and precious, you also, as living stones, are being built up a spiritual house, a holy priesthood, to offer up spiritual sacrifices acceptable to God through Jesus Christ. Therefore it is also contained in the Scripture, Behold, I lay in Zion, a chief cornerstone, elect, precious, And he who believes on Him will by no means be put to shame.

Therefore, to you who believe, He is precious; but to those who are disobedient, The stone which the builders rejected has become the chief cornerstone, And a rock of offense. They stumble, being disobedient to the word, to which they also were appointed.

But you are a chosen generation, a royal priesthood, a holy nation, His own special people, that you may proclaim the praises of Him who called you out of darkness into His marvelous light; who once were not a people but are now the people of God, who had not obtained mercy but now have obtained mercy. Beloved, I beg you as sojourners and pilgrims, abstain from fleshly lusts which war against the soul, having your conduct honorable among the Gentiles, that when they speak against you as evildoers, they may, by your good works which they observe, glorify God in the day of visitation" (1 Pet. 2:2-12). NKJV

Newborns begin to grow as they receive nourishment but they are further developed as they meet and learn to overcome opposition. One of the things believers must overcome is the flesh.

These newborn babes have been accustomed to having things their own way. Their spiritual senses have not yet been sufficiently exercised to discern both good and evil (see Heb. 5:14). They do not yet know they are operating in the flesh. The flesh in the believer must be overcome, but it cannot be overcome until it is isolated and identified.

The word "flesh" is sometimes used to refer to the human body. When so used it does not mean something evil. The physical body itself is neither good nor evil (in the moral sense), but its members (both physical and mental) may be used to accomplish that which is good or evil according to that entity or force which controls it.

The word is also used sometimes to refer to humanity. When used in that sense it may refer to people who are evil, but that is not the emphasis. The flesh we, as believers, must overcome is that in human nature which is inherently evil. This inherited evil is the predisposition to, the inclination toward, and the desire for that which is self enhancing and/ or that which is satisfying to the bodily appetites. This inclination toward and weakness for these things was inherited from our fathers from generation to generation all the way back to Adam. This is stated clearly in Romans chapter five when we read that it was through one man (Adam) that sin entered the world, and that by that one man's disobedience many were made sinners (Rm. 5:12,19).

Even though the word flesh is not mentioned here, we are told that the flesh is the abode and condition in which sin resides and in which it operates. "For when we were in the flesh, the sinful passions which were aroused by the law were at work in our members to bear fruit to death" (Rm. 7:5).

It is well to note here the past tense of the condition, "when we were in the flesh." We (believers) are no longer in the flesh (see also Rom. 8:9). What God has accomplished for us in Christ ends that condition. "For what the law could not do in that it was weak through the flesh, God did by sending His own Son in the likeness of sinful flesh, on account of sin: He condemned sin in the flesh," (Rm. 8:3) (we must return to this entire passage later to find our source of victory).

The term "flesh" then refers to that in our human nature which is predisposed, and which is inclined toward self enhancement or that which is desired to satisfy the bodily appetites. Therefore, whatever in us which meets that description must be overcome. But we find that condition also makes us weak when we attempt to keep the righteous law of God in our strength.

By reviewing briefly the history of mankind, we can see the development of this evil condition called the flesh. Man was created by God and for God (see Col. 1:16). He was God's property created for His purpose. He was obligated to love and serve the Lord his God with all his heart, with all of his mind, with all of his soul, and with all of his strength. Instead, Adam turned from loving and serving God to loving and serving himself. This is evil (perverted) in that God created man upright (Godward) but he perverted his way (turning to himself). This self serving, self pleasing, self determining, self relying condition is the development of the self life (the flesh).

Man's heart, the center and originator of his thoughts and intents, was now turned to self pleasing instead of pleasing his creator and Lord. This condition of self exertion may be expressed in many different ways. It may be expressed as immoral thoughts and actions, as being hurtful or controlling to others, in being cruel, envious of others, jealous of others, etc. or it may come forth as self righteous (presenting ourselves as good) or in being religious, or benevolent (for selfish reasons) etc. Whatever is designed to make us look good, be successful on our own without God, is of the flesh and is sin.

This condition is not limited to the old man, it is present in the believer as well. It is there and must be overcome. There is a very important difference in the condition of the old man and the new man in reference to the flesh. The old man was in it, the cause of it, and under it's persuasion. The new man is under it's influence and it's downward pull affects him (until he overcomes it), but he does not live in it as his natural habitat.

Sin (which operates in the flesh) is also in the new man (see 1 Jn 1:8), but is not of him. Paul wrote, "For when we were in the flesh, the sinful passions which were aroused by the law were at work in our members to bear fruit to death. But now we have been delivered from the law, having died to what we were held by, so that we should serve in the newness of the Spirit and not in the oldness of the letter" (Rm. 7:5,6). When the new man has not come to see this truth and attempts to keep the law in his own strength, putting himself back under the letter of the law, he finds he is unable to do so. His experience will be that as recorded in Romans 7:14-17.

"For we know that the law is spiritual, but I am carnal, sold under sin. For what I am doing, I do not understand. For what I will to do, that I do not practice; but what I hate, that I do. If, then, I do what I will not to do, I agree with the law that it is good. But now, it is no longer I who do it, but sin that dwells in me" (Romans 7:14-17) NKJV

That within man which is self pleasuring, self enhancing, and self promoting, and which opposes spirit life is what the apostle Paul calls "the flesh". This proness toward evil gives sin the openness and opportunity it needs in which to operate. That is where sin is at home.

When Lucifer, son of the morning, became enamored with himself, he gave birth to sin. Now he has infected man with the same condition; sin, which results in death, has entered the world through the heart of man.

The self centered attitude in man is called "flesh" because of its close connection and its outworking through the man's bodily members. The faculties of the soul and the heart are turned toward that which brings pleasure to the bodily appetites and enhances the soul life. This lust which is conceived in the heart as well as its execution in thought, will, affections, and actions is evil.

Man is enslaved to sin because of the weakness of the flesh. This deplorable condition is referred to as "the body of sin" in Romans 6:6. Man's need is twofold: to be free from guilt caused by sinning against God and to overcome the flesh in order to be free from bondage to sin. Being made free from the guilt of sin and then overcoming the flesh are essential to the holy life of the manifest sons of God who are being brought to glory.

The book of Romans reveals what the two fold problem for man is, how we got into the problem, what God has done about the situation, and how the Holy Spirit applies God's solution to the problem. This epistle also tells us that God introduced His law into the situation to make the problem more apparent.

Man's problem, as presented in Romans, is twofold: all men descended from Adam have sinned and are therefore guilty before God (Romans 3:23). Also, all men descended from Adam are sinners. Not only have they sinned but they are enslaved by sin. (Romans 3:9)

Justification by faith is God's solution to the first problem. Justification is the work of God's grace in which He places the ungodly in right standing with Himself on condition of his faith, without works. Abraham illustrates this action of God on behalf of man. Paul says in Romans 4:3-5:

"For what does the Scripture say? Abraham believed God, and it was accounted to him for righteousness. Now to him who works, the wages are not counted as grace but as debt. But to him who does not work but believes on Him who justifies the ungodly, his faith is accounted for righteousness."

David also describes the blessedness of the man to whom God imputes righteousness apart from works:

"Blessed are those whose lawless deeds are forgiven, and whose sins are covered; blessed is the man to whom the Lord shall not impute sin." (Romans 4:6-8)

There are two actions in justifying the ungodly; on the one hand, the sins of the sinner are remitted, while on the other the righteousness of God is put to his account.

This was all done in such a way as not to compromise the nature of God who is absolutely just and therefore, cannot clear the guilty. Payment is required. God's redemptive plan had already been decided. The just would bear the iniquity of the unjust. (1 Pet 3:18)

"Christ also suffered for us, ...who Himself bore our sins in His own body on the tree, that we, having died to sins, might live for righteousness by whose stripes you were healed."(1 Peter 2:21,24) (See also Romans 3:21-28). "Therefore we conclude that a man is justified by faith apart from the deeds of the law."

We can see a definite pattern that develops in the process of justifying the ungodly. First, Christ answers for the sins of the sinner by dying on the cross for them. This allows God, the just Judge, to forgive the sins and absolve the sinner of guilt. This is done in the halls of God's justice making justification possible for any or all sinners who believe.

The second move is to introduce the law of God in order to elevate the nature of sin. It is no longer just violating the conscience of the sinner, but is now transgression of the holy commandment of the creator. It also serves to magnify the grace of God who removes the offense at the expense of His precious Son.

"For until the law sin was in the world, but sin is not imputed when there is no law. Nevertheless death reigned from Adam to Moses, even over these who had not sinned according to the likeness of the transgression of Adam, who is a type of Him who was to come. Moreover the law entered that the offense might abound. But where sin abounded, grace abounded much more." (Romans 5:13,14,20).

The next move according to the pattern is the awakened sinner (under conviction of the Holy Spirit) calling upon the name of the Lord, believing in His name. At that time, "the grace of God and the gift by the grace of the one Man, Jesus Christ, abounds to him." He is absolved of guilt and given the gift of righteousness. This also first takes place in the council of God, at the throne of grace.

The reality of this is registered in the heart of the repentant sinner as the Holy Spirit reveals the things of Christ to him. "He who believes in the Son of God has the witness in himself:" (1John 5:10). "The Spirit Himself bears witness with our spirit that we are children of God." (Romans 8:16).

Romans 5:1-5 gives us the results in the experience of the believer:

"Therefore, having been justified by faith, we have peace with God through our Lord Jesus Christ, through whom also we have access by faith into this grace in which we stand, and rejoice in hope of the glory of God. And not only that, but we also glory in tribulations, knowing that tribulation produces perseverance; and perseverance, character; and character, hope. Now hope does not disappoint, because the love of God has been poured out in our hearts by the Holy Spirit who was given to us." (Romans 5:1-5) NKJV

The second part of man's problem has to do with sin and the flesh. Not only did man commit acts of sin, but he is himself a sinner. Justification solved the problem of sin and guilt, but, if God is to have His man of glory, walking in sanctification and truth, something must be done about the man who has turned to his own way and has become enslaved to sin and Satan.

We will find that the Lord solved the second part of the problem by following the same pattern He followed in solving the first part.

Before we address that subject it will be helpful if we first dismiss a couple of wrong attitudes about how the problem is solved. Some have adopted the position that there is no victory over sin and flesh while we are in this mortal body. We are justified by grace through faith; they say, and therefore it is inevitable that we will continue to commit sins but we can confess our sins and be cleansed by the blood of Christ. This error excuses the believer from pursuing holiness in this life. The Bible, however, not only encourages a life of holiness but commands it.

"For this is the will of God, your sanctification: that you should abstain from sexual immorality; that each of you should know how to possess his own vessel in sanctification and honor, not in passion of lust, like the Gentiles who did not know God; that no one should take advantage of and defraud his brother in this matter, because the Lord is the avenger of all such, as we also forewarned you and testified. For

211

God did not call us to uncleanness, but holiness." (1 Thes. 4:3-7)

This is not to say that believers do not sin and that forgiveness is not available nor that we cannot be cleansed by the blood of Christ if we do sin. It is to say we should not take it lightly if we do sin and that we should (and must) find Gods way of victory over sin and the flesh.

Some of us have embraced another error that promises liberty, but more often produces disappointment and discouragement. This approach teaches from Romans chapter six that there is an old sin nature in us called the old man. This old man of sin within was crucified with Christ. We can achieve victory over this flesh man of sin. A dead man, we are told, does not respond to temptation to sin because he is dead.

If we do sin, they say it is because we have not reckoned (by faith) that we are dead. We need to die to self. By consecrating ourselves completely to God, we come to the place where that old man is crucified and the Holy Spirit gives us the victory through our Lord Jesus Christ.

In spite of how good and how right this sounds, some of us who have diligently tried this approach have found it leads more to self effort and eventual failure rather than rest and victory. Self effort to reckon the old man dead that it may be real in experience does not seem to work because he doesn't stay dead.

There are some questions in this view that need answers. Does the Bible indicate the old man is to be crucified over and over again or is it a once for all incident? Does the Bible identify the old man as the flesh? Is the old man something in the heart of man? If the old man and the flesh are the same thing and if the old man was crucified with Christ in a once for all death, why is the flesh a current and continuous problem, acting contrary to the spirit? When we are exhorted in Scripture to "Likewise you also, reckon yourselves to be dead indeed to sin, but alive to God in Christ Jesus our Lord,"(Romans 6:11), is that to make it so, or because it is so? These questions we will endeavor to answer in our consideration of what the Bible teaches about overcoming the flesh.

Before getting to our subject of this study, (lest this be only an academic exercise of the mind instead of a spiritual experience of entering into heart holiness), let us make the following observation as a sincere precaution.

Our search for biblical truth must be more than an exercise of our mental faculties. In order for spiritual truth to affect the life in a positive way the heart must be involved.

Spiritual truth which comes by revelation of the Holy Spirit comes with faith for implementation, but if the heart is not receptive, the revealed truth is not effective, not being mixed with faith. To illustrate: a person may mentally ascent to the truth that Jesus Christ is the Son of God, that He died for sinners, that He was buried and arose from the dead, and yet that sinner may go on his way unchanged by this life changing message. That person may even shed emotional tears as they see these truths portrayed on screen or stage, may even be incensed that a cruel death should be imposed on such a good, innocent man, and yet not experience a change of heart toward God.

Likewise, a person may accept intellectually the doctrine of justification by faith and yet not repent and believe the gospel.

Brokenness, submissiveness, humility, and meekness will allow the gentle Holy Spirit to lead us into holiness; a haughty, argumentative, attitude will limit Him.

Objective mental appreciation and admiration of spiritual truth impresses the mind; subjective revelation and heart application of spiritual truth is the work of the Holy Spirit.

Now, lest we despair, thinking a life of victory over the flesh and freedom from the law of sin and death are not for us in this life ("For hope deferred makes the heart sick, but when the desire comes, it is a tree of life") (Proverbs 13:12), let us first look at chapter eight of Romans (the victory chapter). Note how confidently Paul exclaims. "There is therefore now no condemnation to those who are in Christ Jesus, who do not walk according to the flesh, but according to the Spirit." (Romans 8:1)

Paul goes on to explain that the superior law of the Spirit of life has overcome the law of sin and death, that, what the law of God could not do, God has done. This was done in and through His Son, and that accomplishment was through the Holy Spirit, and that now the righteousness of the law (holiness of life) might be fulfilled in us.

If that sparks hope in your heart, if you hunger and thirst for righteousness, if your heart answered with Paul, "God forbid" in answer to the question, "shall we continue in sin that grace may abound," and if you are willing to "walk humbly with your God", let us search those three chapters in Romans leading up to chapter eight to find what Paul meant when he said, "there is therefore..." The therefore points to what he has said before.

As we search these verses, let us be willing to lay aside preconceptions and "be swift to hear, slow to speak, slow to wrath…" (let us) lay aside all filthiness and overflow of wickedness, and (let us) receive with meekness the implanted word, which is able to save (our) souls. But (let us) be doers of the word, and not hearers only, deceiving (ourselves). (James 1:19-22)

Let us first recall that we are here in Romans chapters six, seven, and eight, dealing with the solution to the second part of man's problem. In chapters three, four, and five he dealt with the problem of man's sin and guilt, the problem now being dealt with in chapters six, seven and eight is the sinner man himself, and victory over that condition called "flesh". (That inherent inclination toward evil which developed in man when he turned from God Himself in the Garden of Eden)

The same pattern which we found in resolving the first part of man's problem we can find in resolving the second part of the problem. Paul first identified the problem, concluding, "All have sinned and stand guilty before God." Second he tells us how Christ took the sinner's place and paid the debt for redemption by the sacrifice of Himself on the cross, resolving the debt in God's heavenly court. Thirdly he pointed out that the law of God was introduced to amplify the offense, making sin a transgression of God's law to make man more aware of the serious nature of sin. Fourthly the solution to the problem of man's guilt by the gracious sacrifice of His son for His enemies is revealed to repentant sinners by the Holy Spirit. Fifthly, upon repentance and faith of the transgressor, the Holy Spirit makes justification experiential in the life of a believing sinner by witnessing the reality of the things of Christ whereupon the believer is at peace with God and enjoys the other provisions of God's grace. (See Romans 5:1-5)

This same pattern and procedure will bring the solution to the problem next revealed to the believer. The believer, even though justified from the guilt of sins, is not able to perform the righteous requirements of the law. Sin is still able to operate in his members. The question posed in Romans 6:1, "Shall we continue in sin that grace may abound," indicates there is a problem here for the believer.

The problem is expressed more fully in chapter seven,

"For what I will to do, that I do not practice."(Rm. 7:15) AND, "For the good that I will to do, I do not do, but the evil I will not to do, that I practice." (Rm. 7:19)

Even though the new man is joined to Christ in newness of life through the resurrection, He still has a problem with the weakness of the flesh and indwelling sin. Being brought to glory involves overcoming the weakness of the flesh and disabling sin. It is the inherent weakness of the flesh that gives sin the ability to rise up and manifest itself against the law of God when the law commands "you shall not covet" etc.

The very reason the law is involved in the life of the believer is because the life of the believer is out of order. His soul life (psuche) is still exerting itself above the Spirit life (Zoe) in directing the life. This will be explored more in depth later, but because it is the crux of the problem we need to consider it briefly here. Jesus Himself referred to this problem when He spoke of denying self, taking up our cross and following Him, of losing our self life (psuche) in order to keep it unto eternal life (Zoe).

Even though the new man in Christ has problems that must be solved and conditions to overcome concerning sin and flesh, there is a profound difference from when he was the old man in Adam. At that time he is described as being dead in trespasses and in sins, walking according to the course of this world, following the prince of the power of the air, fulfilling the desires of the flesh and of the mind, children of wrath, enslaved to sin, dwelling in the flesh. (See Eph. 2:2,3) (Romans 6:20 and 7:5)

The new man has sin dwelling in him but he is not enslaved to it. The flesh is part of his makeup but he is not in the flesh. (contrast Romans 7:5 with 8:9)

That the old man was centered (dwelling) in the flesh but the new man is not in the flesh but in the spirit is an important and significant distinction. The I myself of the heart of man was centered in satisfying himself when he was the old man. The new man may not be able of himself to fulfill God's will but his heart is turned in that direction. He will be taught of the Lord how to do God's will as he follows on to know the Lord.

The old man was not able to reach the Lord because he was dead in trespasses and in sins. The new man is made alive in Christ by resurrection power, he needs revelation of what that means. (See Paul's prayer in Eph. 1:15-20)

There remains, then, a problem in the new man with indwelling sin and weakness of the flesh even though we have been joined to Christ in resurrection power. Overcoming sin and the weakness of the flesh is part of the development of sons in bringing them to glory.

We have purposely skipped from part one of the pattern which God follows in sanctifying sinners to the third part in order to show how the law serves to make the problem more evident so man will seek more diligently for God's solution. The root of the problem of the new man in Christ not being able to perform the righteousness of God's law is because the man himself is trying to do the work of the law. He is trying to keep the law by his own strength instead of living by the Spirit. He has failed to reckon on the fact that our old man was crucified with Christ in His once for all death to sin that the body of sin might be destroyed. He is acting as though he were still under the law.

"But now we (the new man in Christ) have been delivered from the law, having died to what we were held by, so that we should serve in newness of the Spirit and not in the oldness of the letter." (Romans 7:6)

Let us now return to the second part of God's pattern, that of what Christ did on earth to resolve the problem of man and how it affects the spirituals. We must remember that Christ is the Lamb of God slain from the foundation of the world. What Christ did on earth had already been determined in heaven. When Jesus Christ died on the cross of Calvary, our old man (man created in Adam) was crucified with Him (See Eph. 2:10 and 2 Cor. 5:17). This was all done in the eternal spirit world and is an established fact there. We creatures of time get in on the eternal realities by identification with Christ in His death, burial and resurrection. This is a spiritual reality; the outward testimony to the spiritual reality is baptism. Faith on our part is our response to grace on His part (Romans 6:3,4).

"For by one Spirit we were all baptized into one body whether Jews or Greeks, whether slaves or free and have all been made to drink into one Spirit." (1 Cor.12:13)

"For there are three that bear witness in heaven: the Father, the Word, and the Holy Spirit; and these three are one. And there are three that bear witness on earth: the Spirit, the water, and the blood; and these agree as one." (1 John 5:7, 8)

Death and resurrection is God's way of changing man's status before Him. By the substitutionary death, burial and resurrection of Christ, the sentence of death was carried out on the old sinner, he was buried and a new man resurrected in Christ. Man's status was changed from that of alienated sinners in Adam to that of precious children in Christ. Change in lifestyle occurs as the Holy Spirit renews the mind by application of the truth. Man needed a new relationship with God; God need a new man. The work of Christ has satisfied the need of both.

Paul uses two real life situations to illustrate what has happened. The first is that of being enslaved, or under bondage. When Adam turned from pleasing God to pleasing himself he became flesh, and because of the weakness of the flesh, Adam and all his descendents were, through fear of death, all their lifetime, subject to bondage. (Heb. 2:15)

In order to free these slaves, Jesus, the Son of God, "took flesh and blood, that through death he might destroy him that had the power of death, that is, the devil; and deliver them who through fear of death were all their lifetime subject to bondage." (Heb. 2:14, 15). By taking flesh and the blood, Jesus became man's near kinsman that He might redeem him from bondage.

The price of redemption was death, so Jesus took the place of sinful man and died in his place. Now the debt is paid; the old man has died (being crucified with Christ).

The human race only continued because of the resurrection as the new man in Christ. He is free from the past. Problems arise, however, when this free man does not know what his freedom involves.

Man was freed from the past through the redemption that is in Christ Jesus (See Eph. 1:7). Redemption is a legal transaction involving a contract containing conditions and terms of redemption, requirements of the redeemer, as well as results achieved.

The case we are dealing with (releasing man from the bondages to sin) involves actions here on earth, how that affected the status in heaven and what changes are to be expected within the believer.

God's word, which contains all the qualifications and requirements of redemption, how redemption was accomplished in Christ, and what results may be expected, is settled in heaven forever. It is up to every individual to believe the record God gave of His son. A limited understanding of what the Bible (God's word) teaches about redemption will limit the benefits enjoyed by the believer, and may cause him to remain under, or return to, bondage. That is why Paul admonishes believers to, "Stand fast therefore in the liberty by which Christ has made us free, and do not be entangled again with a yoke of bondage." (Gal. 5:1). "For if I build again those things which I destroyed, I make myself a transgressor. For I through the law died to the law that I might live to God." (Gal. 2:18, 19)

The believer has been completely set free from the bondage of sin, but when he acts as though he must keep the law sin takes advantage of his ignorance and causes him to fail because of the weakness of the flesh.

The second illustration used by the apostle to help us understand what happened as a result of being crucified with Christ is that of marriage. Paul reminds us that the law is binding upon the wife as long as her husband is alive. If the husband dies she is loosed from the law and can be married to another.

This is a problem in that the husband will not die. The wife would be released from the law should she herself die, but then she would be dead. Outside of God her situation is hopeless.

But God, with whom all things are possible, and Who is rich in mercy, arranged to have His Son identify with this pitiable wife, die her death for her, be buried for her, and rise from the dead, bringing her up with Him. Because the old wife died in Him the marriage is ended and the law no longer applies to the new person. She is free from the marriage she was in and is also free to marry another.

If this new resurrected person does not know she is free from that law, she may be deceived into serving her former husband because of the marriage law. Again Paul admonishes, "Therefore, my brethren, you also have become dead to the law through the body of Christ, that you may be married to another to Him who was raised from the dead, that we should bear fruit to God. For when we were in the flesh, the sinful passions which were aroused by the law were at work in our members to bear fruit to death. But now we have been delivered from the law, having died to what we were held by, so that we should serve in newness of Spirit and not in the oldness of the letter." (Romans 7:4-6)

If we have progressed along with Paul in his discussion of how God solves the problem of sin taking advantage of the weakness of the flesh to manifest sin in the new man, we should almost be able to observe the puzzled believer as he taps his temple with his index finger while a small light bulb (or oil lamp) lights up over his head as he muses, "Hmmm, If I delight in the law of God in my inner man, but when I will to do it, sin happens, it is not me (my inner man) doing it, it is sin doing it through my flesh. I see, then, this law working against my mind bringing me into captivity. Who will deliver me from this condition? Christ Jesus my Lord! I now see what is wrong, it is I myself working, using my mind to keep the law, and the flesh causes me to fail."

(If you consider this an oversimplification of these verses or a perversion of what Paul is saying, let us take a quick look at Galatians 2:18-21 where Paul is confronting the Judaisers who have gone out teaching that faith alone is not enough, we must also be circumcised and keep the law. In verse 18 Paul has come to the conclusion of his argument, "For if I build again these things I destroyed, I make myself a transgressor," This in response to what he saw that, "they (the followers of Christ. Peter, Barnabas, and others who had fallen into the error of the law observer) were not straightforward about the truth of the gospel," (vs.14) but had reversed themselves. They had laid Judaism (seeking justification by keeping the law) aside, taking their place with Gentile sinners in order to be justified by faith in Christ. By turning back they had transgressed the law of faith.

Paul then presents the truth of the gospel. "For I through the law died to the law that I might live to God. I have been crucified with Christ; it is no longer I who live, but Christ lives in me; and the life which I now live in the flesh I live by faith in the Son of God (or better: in the faith of the Son of God), who loved me and gave Himself for me. I do not set aside the grace of God; for if righteousness comes through the law, then Christ died in vain. "(Gal. 2:18-21). My self efforts frustrate the Grace of God.

The life described here is not Paul living his life for God, nor is it Christ living Paul's life through him; it is Christ living His own life through the life of the apostle.

By denying himself the throne, taking up his cross (putting to death the deeds of the body by the Spirit) (Romans 8:13) following Christ (letting Him lead), losing his soul life, he keeps it unto eternal (spirit) life. His soul (psuche) is now in its rightful place, subservient to his spirit in order that the Holy Spirit is allowed to make the Christ life experiential within the believer.

Let us see this in Paul's illustration in the slave who was freed from bondage to sin. He was not freed to serve himself. He will serve one master or another. He must now choose to serve God by yielding his members to Him to bring forth fruit unto holiness, not trying to serve God by keeping the law in his own strength.

And as for the wife who dies to her husband and also to the law of marriage, she is now free to legally marry the One who died and rose again to bring forth fruit unto God. (Romans 7:14)

There are some things that are true in a Biblical marriage relationship that we may have lost sight of in modern marriage. In a Biblical marriage: The wife gave up her life for his, taking his name. the husband gave himself up for her, taking responsibility for her. The husband was her head, leading her. The wife submitted herself to him, following him.

A marriage in God's order is impervious to the enemy. Had Adam been in his place and Eve in hers the enemy could not have gotten to her.

The life of victory over sin in the believer is not one of continually struggling to reckon the old self within us dead indeed unto sin so we can experience it. It is rather a life of resting in Christ and faith in His accomplishments in the cross.

Through His accomplishments we are both the righteousness of God in Him and He is made unto us sanctification as well (See 1 Cor. 1:30). We know that we are set apart (sanctified-made holy) when we are baptized into Christ by the Holy Spirit. Everything in Christ is set apart to God, therefore holy unto Him. However, there is a work within the believer whereby the very nature of the believer is changed, producing holiness of life.

Think how wonderful this is. The believer is instantly and continuously righteous before the Judge (seeing it is the Judge Himself who gave him the gift of His own righteousness) and then by the indwelling Holy Spirit he is made holy and godly in daily life experience. He is made partaker of the divine nature (See 2 Peter 1:2-4).

This experience is not automatic for every believer. This life experience is available to every believer, but one must enter it by faith. This entrance may be initiated by a crisis, greater for some, lesser for others, depending upon how strong the self life is in each. To bring one who is strong and talented in leadership skills, and who has achieved a position or recognition among people, to the point of having "no reputation" (See Phil. 2:5-15) may require severe dealings. To bring those who, by their own ingenuity or business accumen have amassed great wealth, to the place where they would give it all up and depend upon the Lord to sustain them may likewise require severe measure.

But if we would walk this holy walk with Him, we must "forsake all". By one means or another we must be brought to the point of desperation where we hunger and thirst for righteousness. For some it may be out of love and a sincere desire to please Him. Others may have to be hemmed up in "wits-end-alley". It is only those who cry out with the man in Romans seven, "O wretched man that I am! who shall deliver me from the body of this death", to whom the Holy Spirit can reveal the way of deliverance.

The work has already been done as far as heaven's court is concerned. "For what the law could not do in that it was week through the flesh, God did by sending His own Son in the likeness of sinful flesh, on account of sin: He condemned sin in the flesh, that the righteous requirement of the law might be fulfilled in us who do not walk according to the flesh but according to the Spirit." (Romans 8:3, 4)

Whatever was needed to make it possible for us to walk in victory was accomplished in Christ. We experience it by following the Holy Spirit. As we set our attention (minds) on the Holy Spirit, He is able to do in and through us whatever the Father wants done. That is exactly the way Jesus worked while on earth. He said he did nothing except what He saw the Father doing. He kept His attention on the Father. That doesn't mean He stood around constantly gazing into heaven. It is true His Father was in heaven, but He was also inside Jesus. He said to Philip, "Do you not believe that I am in the Father, and the Father in me?" (John 14:10). The way Jesus saw what the Father was doing was by "looking" into His own spirit where the Father was residing.

We, as believers, have the Spirit of Christ dwelling within our spirits (See Romans 8:9-11). We must see the liberty we have in Christ by revelation of the Holy Spirit. We begin this victorious life by surrendering ourselves up to Him to walk by faith in Him alone. We have no confidence in the flesh. We continue this walk by paying attention (setting our minds) on the Spirit who is alive within our hearts. (see Rm. 8:5-13)

Have you seen this truth by revelation of the Holy Spirit? Then enter without delay. With the revelation comes the faith to obey.

Chapter Twelve

The Devil We Overcome

O vercoming is not optional for believers, it is expected. If overcoming were not possible, God would not expect it. The long list of the faithful mentioned in Hebrews chapter eleven are all overcomers. All of them met obstacles in their journey and came out victorious. Their victories were not all achieved in the same way. Some went over their adversities, some went through and some went down, but all overcame by their faith in the Lord; they would not deny Him.

From a worldly perspective, we are more likely to think of "those who through faith subdued kingdoms, worked righteousness, obtained promises, stopped the mouths of lions, quenched the violence of fire, escaped the edge of the sword, out of weakness were made strong, became valiant in battle, turned to flight the armies of the aliens, women received their dead raised to life again." (Heb. 11:33-35) as successful overcomers while discounting the, "Others (who) were tormented, not accepting deliverance, that they might obtain a greater resurrection. (and) still others (who) had trial of cruel mocking and scourging, yes, and of chains and imprisonment. They were stoned; they were slain with the sword. They wandered about in sheepskin and goatskins, being destitute, afflicted, tormented", and yet it was these of whom it is said, "Of whom the world was not worthy" (Heb. 11:35-38). All of these (all these groups) obtained a good testimony by faith.

There is a real living spirit being with whom we are all sure to deal at some point in our journey, and one whom we must overcome. He is called the devil (traducer, false accuser, and slanderer). He is also called Satan (accuser). Peter refers to him as "your adversary, saying, "Be sober, be vigilant because your adversary, the devil walks about like a roaring lion, seeking whom he may devour. Resist him, steadfast in the faith, knowing that the same sufferings are experienced by your brotherhood in the world." (1 Peter 5:8, 9)

This spirit being is also called "That old serpent of old" in Revelation 12:9, identifying him as the being who deceived Eve and tempted Adam in the Garden of Eden.

In the passage in Revelation 12 he is also called "the great dragon" (called the Devil and Satan) who, with his angels, was involved in a war against the archangel Michael and his angels in heaven. The dragon lost the war and was cast out into the earth with his angels. It is said of him that he accuses the brethren before our God day and night.

This spirit being was created by God as Lucifer. He was created a very beautiful creature who could make beautiful music from his very being. Evidently he led the angelic beings in giving praise to God.

And then, iniquity developed in his own heart. He became enamored with his own beauty, became filled with pride and rebelled against God. That is when he became God's adversary.

He was jealous of man who was created in the image and likeness of God with the great destiny of ruling with God. The adversary of God became the adversary of man and began to slander him before God. Because sin had now entered man, the devil could accuse man before God. Even though God has, by His grace, justified sinful man, the enemy continues to accuse him before God, and, in man's conscience.

The character of the devil can be described in words like: proud, wicked, subtle, rebellious, dishonest, fierce, cruel, and presumptuous. He is a lying deceiver who is opposed to God. He desires to steal, kill and destroy. We, as children of God must overcome his influence in our lives as well as be victorious against his schemes.

A good question to ponder is why the devil is still allowed to roam around on earth heckling God's children. There is a reason for it at this time. He will not do this forever; his end has already been written. He has already lost his position in heaven. His power on earth is limited both in jurisdiction and in duration.

Satan had the power of death (See Heb. 2:14) but when Jesus arose from the dead He took the authority (key) of hell and of death (Rev. 1:18).

Both Satan and this world system were judged when they put Jesus to death. (How wondrous and far reaching is that cross!) Jesus, when drawing near the time of His death, said "Now is the judgment of this world; now the ruler of this world will be cast out." John 12:31). Satan's doom is sealed. Both he and his followers have been condemned.

The cross stands in history and in the spirit realm as a demarcation of those who are for God and those who are opposed to Him. There is a war on at this present time for the minds of men. All men have the choice of yielding to God at the cross of Christ or continuing in their own way.

The battle rages as we make known the knowledge of God to men's minds. "We wrestle not against flesh and blood, but against principalities, against powers, against spiritual hosts of wickedness in the heavenly places." (Eph. 6:12). "For (but) though we walk in the flesh, (fleshly bodies), we do not war according to the flesh. For the weapons of our warfare are not carnal but mighty in God for pulling down strongholds, casting down arguments and every high thing that exalts itself against the knowledge of God, bringing every thought into captivity to the obedience of Christ." (2 Cor. 10:3-5).

We bring the light of Christ; man must make the decision whether or not to walk in the light. Eventually the battle between light and darkness will culminate in the battle of Armageddon where the forces of Satan, under allegiance to the man of sin (the antichrist), will be arrayed against the Lord and His Christ to oppose the coming of His kingdom of righteousness to be established on earth. The Lord Jesus will annihilate the armies of the antichrist, the antichrist and the false prophet who supported him will be cast into the abyss. Satan will be bound for one thousand years, then released for a short time and eventually be cast into the abyss where the beast (antichrist) and false prophet are.

To know the reason for loosing Satan for a short time after the one thousand years is to know why he is loose today. During those one thousand years, while Christ reigns on earth, natural people will be born. God created man with the ability of choice on purpose. Only those who choose to love God and serve Him willingly will be included in His eternal kingdom. Satan is loosed to deceive the nations of natural people on earth. Those who choose the selfish, self centered way of Satan will be cast into the abyss with him.

That helps us to understand why God allows Satan to roam earth today. Those who would serve God must choose to do so. We are here to help open their eyes to the truth so they make the choice on their own accord without Satan imposing blindness on their eyes.

We, as believers, learn to overcome Satan and his wiles by "putting on the Lord Jesus Christ, (making) no provision for the flesh, to fulfill its lusts." (See Romans 13:8-14). "Finally, my brethren, be strong in the Lord and in the power of His might. Put on the whole armor of God, that you may be able to stand against the wiles of the devil." (Eph. 6:10-11 and following).

The Lord Jesus overcame the devil in His life. He will do the same by His life in me. We must not neglect the means by which this is done, "praying always with all prayer and supplication in the Spirit, being watchful to this end with all perseverance and supplication for all the saints." (Eph. 6:18).

We must take seriously the admonition of Jesus to "watch and pray, lest you enter into temptation. The spirit indeed is willing, but the flesh is weak." (Mt. 26:41).

How did Jesus (as a man) overcome the devil? (It would be no problem at all for God to overcome the devil, one word [or even a glance] could annihilate any or all created beings) But Jesus overcame the enemy in His humanity.

Jesus was purposely led out into the desert (wilderness of Judea) to be tempted of the devil.

"Then Jesus was led up by the Spirit into the wilderness to be tempted by the devil. And when He had fasted forty days and forty nights, afterward He was hungry. Now when the tempter came to Him, he said, "If You are the Son of God, command that these stones become bread." But He answered and said, "It is written, 'Man shall not live by bread alone, but by every word that proceeds from the mouth of God.'"

Then the devil took Him up into the holy city, set Him on the pinnacle of the temple, and said to Him, "If You are the Son of God, throw Yourself down. For it is written: 'He shall give His angels charge over you,' and, 'In their hands they shall bear you up, Lest you dash your foot against a stone.'" Jesus said to him, "It is written again, 'You shall not tempt the LORD your God.'" Again, the devil took Him up on an exceedingly high mountain, and showed Him all the kingdoms of the world and their glory. And he said to Him, "All these things I will give You if You will fall down and worship me." Then Jesus said to him, "Away with you, Satan! For it is written, 'You shall worship the LORD your God, and Him only you shall serve.'" Then the devil left Him, and behold, angels came and ministered to Him." (Mt. 4:1-11) NKJV

The devil approached Jesus at the point of His greatest physical need, at the moment He was physically hungry because He had been fasting for forty days and forty nights. There are two distinct parts to this particular temptation: first, "if you are the Son of God…" By taking action to prove He was the Son of God, Jesus would actually be questioning whether He was the Son of God in truth. The truth itself is all the proof required. Had Jesus obeyed Satan, He would have been submitting to his strategy. Eve, in the garden of Eden, fell into Satan's trap; Jesus did not.

The second part of the temptation was to act independently of His Father, to supply His own need. Jesus answered the devil's solicitation by giving him the word of God. We also overcome the devil with the sword of the Spirit – the word of God.

The second temptation had to do wth drawing attention to himself for self glory. This temptation is also in two parts; the first part is to question the validity of the word of God by attempting to prove it by putting it to the test. We prove the word of God is true by simply obeying it, not demonstrating it for show. When we attempt to prove God by putting Him to thc test we inadvertently draw attention and glory to ourselves.

The third temptation is to give allegiance to and to worship Satan. Jesus overcame the devil in each case by giving him the word of God. Since the word of God is the sword of the Spirit (see Eph. 6:17), the Holy Spirit gave Jesus the appropriate word at the time needed. He will do the same for each of us. Jesus did not merely quote verses to Satan, He spoke the word to him with authority.

Being rebuffed; Satan left Jesus for a time. (see Lk. 4:13). He would return to tempt Jesus in every way man is tempted, by every conceivable means possible, and with all his subtlety, but Jesus never gave in to him in any way, to any degree. Christ in us will do the same if we are surrendered and attentive to Him.

The procedure we must use in overcoming Satan is in Rev. 12:11, "and they overcame him by the blood of the Lamb and by the word of their testimony, and they did not love their lives to the death."

The blood of the Lamb frees the believer from the guilt and consequence of sin, therefore the accuser has nothing to accuse us of that will bring condemnation.

The word of our testimony is the word of God and our faith in it. It is ours only because we believe it and testify it to Satan. He knows the word is true and he knows whether or not we believe it.

What can he do to us if we believe the word of God enough that we lay our lives down for it, having no confidence in the flesh. When we love God and His word more than our own lives we have overcome the devil.

Chapter Thirteen

Where God is All in All

Jesus is God's anointed. In Hebrew the word is <u>Messiah</u>; in Greek it is <u>Christ</u>. If we underestimate what it means to be God's anointed, we will not be able to understand what God had in mind from the beginning.

God's anointed is more than the deliverer, to free the oppressed Jews. He is more than Abraham's Seed, inheriting the covenant promises. He is more than our Savior, to save us from our sins. Yes, He is all of that, Praise God forever, but He is so much more.

When we begin to understand what Paul meant when he spoke of, "the mystery of His will, according to His good pleasure which He purposed in Himself, that in the dispensation of the fullness of the times He might gather together in one all things in Christ (the anointed), both which are in heaven and which are on earth – in Him." (Eph 1:9,10) When we begin to get a glimpse of what it means that God purposed that everything (can we grasp it? EVERYTHING except God Himself) is to be under the headship of Jesus, God's Anointed, then we will begin to see what God had in mind from the beginning.

We humans are so egocentric so earth-minded, we see everything from our earth perspective. Will we ever understand that the universe did not begin with us? The Holy Spirit helps us to see reality from the eternal spiritual perspective when He says through the apostle Paul, "He (Jesus - God's Anointed) is the image of the invincible God, the firstborn over all creation.

"For by Him all things were created that are in heaven and that are on earth, visible and invisible, whether thrones or dominions or principalities or power. All things were created through Him and for Him. And He is before all things, and in Him all things consist. And He is the head of the body, the church, who is the beginning, the firstborn from the dead, that in all things He may have the preeminence. For it pleased

the Father that in Him all the fullness should dwell."
(Col. 1:15-19).

Jesus is God's ULTIMATE MAN, the MAN which He intended from the beginning. Since we are in Him, we also are anointed for God's eternal purpose. We are included in His purpose.

The book of Revelations, being "the revelation of Jesus Christ" (Rev. 1:1), gives us some idea of what happens to bring everything on earth under Him. The revelation (unveiling) was given to the apostle John in symbolic language, (he signified it Rev. 1:1). Not everything in the book is symbolical, but much of it is.

Some of the events and things revealed are in heaven, in the spiritual realm. Our minds cannot comprehend these things., nor could they be expressed in natural terms. Because there are no natural words which could convey the meaning, He expressed it in symbols and picture language. Some of these revelations are things that would happen in the future. To retain the necessity of the imminency of His return, He signified it, because, had He given it to us in natural terms we would know these things would not happen until many generations had come and gone. The time of His coming must be kept imminent lest believers become complacent about it. Some things may be revealed in natural terms but some must be symbolized.

We cannot here explore the entire book of Revelation but we will look at a few of the things that reveal Jesus Christ as He brings things on earth under His headship.

In chapter four we read that John saw a door standing open into heaven and was called to come up there. Immediately John was in the spirit and saw One sitting upon a magnificent throne and heard four living creatures saying:

"Holy, holy, holy, Lord God Almighty who was and is and is to come!"

John then saw the twenty four elders, who were around the throne, cast their crowns before the throne saying;

"You are worthy, O Lord, to receive glory and honor and power; For you created all things."

John saw in the right hand of Him who sat on the throne a scroll, written on the inside and on the back, sealed with seven seals. This scroll is of paramount importance because the content revealed when the seals are loosed consumes most of the rest of the Book of Revelation. So important is this scroll that John wept much when no one in heaven was found worthy to open the seals of the scroll or to even look at it.

What is this scroll, who is qualified to open it and what is the significance of opening the seals? Some consider the scroll to be the Book of Revelations itself but that seems unlikely since the book contains scenes and events before and after the opening of the seals.

There are other references to sealed documents in the Scriptures. By examining one of these references in Jeremiah Chapter 32 and 33 we may be able to get insight into this one in Revelation chapter five. They are similar in that both have an open part and a sealed part. (Please read these amazing chapters in Jeremiah and marvel at the faithfulness of our covenant keeping God, and revel in His longsuffering, goodness and mercy In His loving kindness (grace) toward His people, the unfaithful Jews.

The scenario in Jeremiah is that Jerusalem is under siege by Nebuchadnezzar king of Babylon. Jeremiah the prophet is imprisoned in the court of the prison in the king of Judah's house. Zedekiah, king of Judah, had Jeremiah imprisoned because he had prophesied that unfaithful Judah, including

Zedekiah the king, would be led captive to Babylon. The land of promise which God had given them in His covenant with Abraham would be confiscated by their ungodly enemies.

While Jeremiah was in prison, the word of the Lord came to him that his uncle's son Hanamel would come to him asking him to exercise his right of redemption to purchase the land of his father. The Lord instructed Jeremiah to buy the land in expectancy of the eventual return of His people to reposses their land. He was to sign the deed in the presence of witnesses. The witnessed deed was in two parts; one was to be open, the other sealed. The signed witnessed deed; both the proof of purchase deed which was sealed and that which was open, were to be put in an earthen vessel to be kept many days.

We cannot speak definitely what was contained in the deed. We can surmise that, according to covenant documents, it would contain proof of purchase and terms of redemption.

We will compare this scenario to what John saw in heaven. One of the elders told John there was no need to weep, "Behold, the Lion of the tribe of Judah, the Root of David, has prevailed to open the scroll and loose its seven seals: (Rev. 5:5).

We know by this, and by what follows, the scroll pertains to earth. The twenty four elders fall down and worship the Lord singing this new song;

"You are worthy to take the scroll
And to open its seals;
For you were slain,
And have redeemed us to God
By Your blood
Out of every tribe and tongue,
And people, and nation
And have made us kings and priests
To our God;
And we shall reign on earth."
(Revelation 5:9,10)

These worshipers had golden bowls in their hands which contained over two thousand years of the prayers of the saints. The essence of these prayers were, no doubt,

"Our Father, which art in heaven, Hallowed be Thy name. Thy kingdom come, Thy will be done on earth as it is in heaven." (Mt. 6:9, 10)

248

The reference the elders made to redemption reminds us of Jesus as our Kinsman Redeemer. Jesus is qualified in every respect to be man's Kinsman Redeemer. Seeing Him as a Lamb with marks of having been slain reminds us that Jesus is the Lamb of God who takes away the sins of the world. Hearing the elder refer to Him as the Lion of the tribe of Judah, the Root of David, reminds us that Jesus is to sit as King on David's throne and reign in righteousness on earth. One of these refers to Him dying in weakness; the other of His coming in power and great splendor.

The Kinsman Redeemer could redeem both persons and property. In the case of an indentured person, the redeemer may pay what was owed and release the indentured from servitude. In the case of lost property the redeemer may pay an earnest amount, sign the necessary proof of purchase and return later to take the possession of his purchase.

Not only must the Kinsman Redeemer be qualified as a near kinsman, he must also be willing to pay the debt owed by the indentured or against the property, and be able to release the purchase from any and all encumbrances that may exist, but he must also be able to legally depose any usurper who has laid claim to the possession.

The Lion of the tribe of Judah, the Root of David, in preparing to take possession of His purchase, takes the scroll (perhaps the title deed to all that Adam lost, containing terms and conditions of possession) from the hand of Him who sat on the throne. He, and He alone, is worthy to take the scroll (His legally certified title deed) and open its seven seals. The Father Himself has certified the purchase, having approved the payment of life blood, and has conveyed upon Him the right to reign.

When the Lamb opens the seals cataclysmic events take place on earth and in heaven. These events cause mixed reactions among the people of earth; some in desperation call upon the name of the Lord and are saved while others curse God and cry out to the rocks and mountains to fall on them to hide them from the face of Him who sits on the throne and from the wrath of the Lamb (See Rev. Chapter 6).

We know many are saved during this time, and, as a result of these events because when John saw a great multitude which no man could number out of all nations, tribes, peoples and tongues, standing before the throne and before the Lamb, clothed in white robes with palm branches in their hands, crying with loud voices, "Salvation belongs to our

God who sits on the throne and to the Lamb" he was told these came out of the great tribulation (See Rev. 7:9-17).

These events continue through the blowing of the fourth trumpet (included in the seventh seal) when an angel flying through the midst of heaven announces three woes by reason of the three trumpets which are yet to sound (Rev. 8:13).

The first woe, at the blowing of the fifth trumpet, is the release of a horde of (apparently) demonic locusts to torment men for five months so horribly they cry to die but are not allowed to.

The second woe involves the release of four angels in the middle east whose assignment is to kill one third part of mankind. By comparing Rev. 9:13-19 with Rev. 16:12-16, it might be that this visitation of wrath includes the battle of Armageddon.

The third woe has to do with the return of our Lord Jesus to the earth wherein the kingdom of this world becomes the kingdom of our Lord and of His Christ. (See Rev. 12:14-19). The coming of the Lord also involves His intervention to defeat the armies who are arrayed against Him at Armageddon and also destroying the Babylonian world system.

Even after the salvation of multitude and violent and horrible death of many others, the remainder of earth dwellers remain unrepentant. (See Rev. 11:20, 21). This had been foretold by David in the Psalms:

"Your hand will find all your enemies; your right hand will find those who hate you. You shall make them as a fiery oven in the time of your anger; the Lord shall swallow them up in His wrath, and the fire shall devour them. Their offspring you shall destroy from the earth, and their descendants from among the sons of men. For they intended evil against you; they devised a plot which they are not able to perform. Therefore you will make them turn their back; you will ready your arrows on your string toward their faces." (Ps. 21:8-12)

The ridiculous plot which these devil inspired leaders devised is described in the second Psalm.

"Why do the nations rage and the people plot a vain thing? The kings of the earth set themselves, and the rulers take counsel together, against the Lord and against His anointed saying, Let us break their bonds in pieces, and cast away their cords from us." (Ps. 2:1-3)

The Lord laughs at the absurd thought that men, even devil inspired men could resist Almighty God! He simply announces:

"Yet I have set My King on My holy hill of Zion. I will declare the decree: You are My Son, Today I have begotten you. Ask of me and I will give you the nations for your inheritance, and the ends of the earth for your possession. You shall break them with a rod of iron; you shall dash them to pieces like a potter's vessel." (Ps. 2:6-9)

Jesus, in His coming, destroys the antichrist, the false prophet and the armies that followed them. He also sets His hand to destroy the Babylonian world system that devils and men have imposed upon the earth, which consists of political, religious and commercial organizations. The system collapses mostly from within. Nevertheless, it is the Lord who gives it the cup of the fierceness of His wrath which causes the destruction (Rev. 16:19).

From Mount Zion in Jerusalem Jesus reigns over the nation of Israel and those who did not take sides with the antichrist. He reigns for one thousand years until all enemies are put under His feet.

Jesus, as Son of Man, reigns on earth in order that God's unconditional promises may be fulfilled:

1) The promise to remove the curse from the earth - through the Seed of the woman (Gen. 3:15)

2) The promise to bless all families of the earth - through the Seed of Abraham (Gen. 12:2, 3)

3) The promise to Israel of the land as an everlasting possession - through Messiah (Gen. 48:4; Is. 11:10, 11; Jer. 32:38-43)

4) The promise to David, that his seed would be established to sit on his throne –through the Lion of Judah, the Root of David forever (Ps. 89:3, 4; Hos. 3:5; Acts 15:16)

5) The promise to the Son of Man "that at the name of Jesus every knee should bow, of those in heaven, those on earth, and those under the earth, and that

every tongue should confess that Jesus Christ is Lord, to the glory of God the Father." (Phil. 2:10, 11)

Jesus must reign until all enemies are under His feet:

"Then comes the end, when He delivers the kingdom to God the Father, when He puts an end to all rule and all authority and power. For he must reign till He has put all enemies under His feet. The last enemy that will be destroyed is death.

Now when all things are made subject to Him, then the Son Himself will also be subject to Him who put all things under Him, that God may be All in All." (1 Cor. 15:24-26, 28)

When Christ is reigning on the throne of His glory, those who have suffered with Him, and who have overcome, will reign with Him in glory. When all enemies are under His feet, when nature has been delivered from its groaning and restored to its original glory, when His church is filled with the glory of God, and every creature willingly submitted to the Father's will - then everything will be swallowed up in

Him. God will be all in all; we in Christ, Christ in us; Christ in God, God in Christ!

Let us then, "present our bodies a living sacrifice, holy, acceptable to God, (that we may) be transformed by the renewing of (our) mind, that (we) may prove what is that good and acceptable and perfect will of God."(Romans 12:1, 2)

"The night is far spent, the day is at hand. Therefore let us cast off the works of darkness, and let us put on the full armor of light. Let us walk properly, as in the day not in revelry and drunkenness, not in lewdness and lust, not in strife and envy. But (let us) put on the Lord Jesus Christ, and make no provision for the flesh, to fulfill its lusts." (Romans 13:12-14)

And let us accept the prayer of the apostle Paul (as it is of the Holy Spirit) as for us:

"For this reason I bow my knees to the Father of our Lord Jesus Christ, from whom the whole family in heaven and earth is named, that He would grant you, according to the riches of His glory, to be strengthened with might through His Spirit in the inner man, that Christ may dwell in your hearts through faith; that you, being rooted and grounded in love, may be able to comprehend with all the saints what is the width and length and depth and height – to know the love of Christ which passes knowledge; that you may be filled with all the fullness of God. Now to Him who is able to do exceedingly abundantly above all that we ask or think, according to the power that works in us, to Him be the glory in the church by Christ Jesus to all generations, forever and ever. Amen." (Eph. 3:14-21)

Sons who are glorified with the glory of Christ will reign with Him over the works of God's hands. What that will mean is beyond description. We can know the reality of it by revelation of the Holy Spirit.

Even with all his modern technology, man has not been able to discover nor to describe the expanse of God's created universe, how much less are we able to comprehend the creator. Words fail, the imagination exhausted, and the heart trembles at any attempt to express the awe and wonder of such a marvelous being as is revealed in the Bible. He is more than wonderful, more than marvelous. He is awesome, and yet He invites us to know Him personally, to communicate with Him and to love Him!

We are destined by Him to share in His glory, to participate with Him over the works of His hands, to be one with Him.

In the glorious eternal day He will be all in all. We will be absorbed into Him, and yet we retain our identity. We will be complete in Christ and He completed by us. We will be in Christ, and He in us. He will be in the Father and the Father in Him. God will have His man, and we will have our God.

This is beyond comprehension, but not beyond faith. God will be all and in all!

To Him be the glory both now and forever!

THE ONE IN YOU

The One in you is faithful
The One in you is true
He is in you Almighty God
And all things He can do

So let Him live His life in you
And He will make you holy
Then you will be among the few
Whose life will bring Him glory

The One in you is righteous
The One in you is just
He is in you the great I AM
In Him only can you trust

So let Him live His life in you
And He will make you holy
Then you will be among the few
Whose life will bring Him glory

The One in you is lovely
The One in you is good
He is in you both King and Lord
Do you know Him as you should

Oh, let Him live His life in you
And He will make you holy
Then you will be among the few
Whose life will bring Him glory

Lynda Gardner

Breinigsville, PA USA
10 March 2011
257367BV00005B/88/P